I Could Tell You Stories

Also by Patricia Hampl

PROSE

A Romantic Education
Virgin Time
Spillville
(with engravings by Steven Sorman)

POETRY

Resort and Other Poems
Women Before an Aquarium

AS EDITOR

Burning Bright: An Anthology of Sacred Poetry

Sojourns

in the Land

of Memory

I Could Tell You Stories

Patricia Hampl

W. W. NORTON & COMPANY

NEW YORK | LONDON

First published as a Norton paperback 2000

For information about permission to reproduce selections from
this book, write to Permissions, W. W. Norton & Company,
500 Fifth Avenue, New York, NY 10110

Credit for works cited in the text can be found on page 233.

The text of this book is composed in Bembo
Composition by Platinum Manuscript Services
Manufacturing by The Maple-Vail Book Manufacturing Group
Book design and photo by Judith Stagnitto Abbate

Library of Congress Cataloging-in-Publication Data

Hampl, Patricia (date).
I could tell you stories : sojourns in the land
of memory / Patricia Hampl
p.   cm.
Includes bibliographical references.
ISBN 0-393-04738-5
1. Biography as a literary form. 2. Autobiographical memory.
3. Autobiography. 4. Hampl, Patricia, (date). I. Title.
CT21 .H33 1999
818'.5409—dc21
[b]
98-51839
CIP

ISBN 0-393-32031-6 pbk.

W. W. Norton & Company, Inc.
500 Fifth Avenue, New York, N.Y. 10110
www.wwnorton.com

W. W. Norton & Company Ltd.
10 Coptic Street, London WC1A 1PU

1 2 3 4 5 6 7 8 9 0

For

Jonathan, Stephen,

and Peter Williams

Contents

To the Reader

A writer is, first and last, a reader. Who do you write for? Gertrude Stein was asked, and famously replied, "Myself and strangers." That self, the reader-self who is allied with strangers, may be a writer's better half, more detached, more trustworthy, than the writing self who swaggers through a lifetime of prose. It is difficult—and diminishing—to separate the self who writes from the one who reads. Both acts belong to the communion of the word, which is a writer's life.

This collection moves back and forth between memoirs with stories that tell about the writing of a life, and the surprisingly passionate experience of a reader trying to tease out from the works of others the habits of memory as it flares into the imagination.

Jean-Paul Sartre organized his luminous memoir, *The Words,* into two parts: "Reading" and "Writing," as if to say that all of life falls into these two camps. A bookish division of reality, perhaps. But then, writers write about writing and about books not because, like us, books turn to dust, but because, like us, they are born of flesh, and you can feel the blood beat along their pulse.

I Could Tell You
Stories

Red Sky
in the Morning

Years ago, in another life, I woke to look out the smeared window of a Greyhound bus I had been riding all night, and in the still-dark morning of a small Missouri river town where the driver had made a scheduled stop at a grimy diner, I saw below me a stout middle-aged woman in a flowered housedress turn and kiss full on the mouth a godlike young man with golden curls. But I've got that wrong: *he* was kissing *her.* Passionately, without regard for the world and its incomprehension. He had abandoned himself to his love, and she, stolid, matronly, received this adoration with simple grandeur, like a socialist-realist statue of a woman taking up sheaves of wheat.

Their ages dictated that he must be her son, but I had just come out of the cramped, ruinous half sleep of a night on a Greyhound and I was clairvoyant: This was that thing called love. The morning light cracked blood red along the river.

Of course, when she lumbered onto the bus a moment later, lurching forward with her two bulging bags, she chose the empty aisle seat next to me as her own. She pitched one bag onto the overhead rack, and then heaved herself into the seat as if she were used to hoisting sacks of potatoes onto the flatbed of a pickup. She held the other bag on her lap, and leaned toward the window. The beautiful boy was blowing kisses. He couldn't see where she was in the dark interior, so he blew kisses up and down the side of the bus, gazing ardently at the blank windows. "Pardon me," the woman said without looking at me, and leaned over, bag and all, to rap the glass. Her beautiful boy ran back to our window and kissed and kissed, and finally hugged himself, shutting his eyes in an ecstatic pantomime of love-sweet-love. She smiled and waved back.

Then the bus was moving. She slumped back in her seat, and I turned to her. I suppose I looked transfixed. As our eyes met she said, "Everybody thinks he's my son. But he's not. He's my husband." She let that sink in. She was a farm woman with hands that could have been a man's; I was a university student, hair down to my waist. It was long ago, as I said, in another life. It was even another life for the country. The Vietnam War was the time we were living through, and I was traveling, as I did every three weeks, to visit my boyfriend who was in a federal prison. "Draft dodger," my brother said. "Draft resister," I piously retorted. I had never been kissed the way this woman had been kissed. I was living in a tattered corner of a romantic idyll, the one where the hero is willing to suffer for his beliefs. I was the girlfriend. I lived on pride, not love.

My neighbor patted her short cap of hair, and settled in for the long haul as we pulled onto the highway along the river, heading south. "We been married five years and we're happy," she said with a penetrating satisfaction, the satisfaction that passeth understanding. "Oh," she let out a profound sigh as if she mined her truths from the bountiful, bulky earth, "Oh, I could tell you stories." She put her arms snugly around her bag, gazed off for a moment, apparently made pensive by her remark. Then she closed her eyes and fell asleep.

I looked out the window smudged by my nose which had been pressed against it at the bus stop to see the face of true love reveal itself. Beyond the bus the sky, instead of becoming paler with the dawn, drew itself out of a black line along the Mississippi into an alarming red flare. It was very beautiful. The old caution—*Red sky in the morning, sailor take warning*—darted through my mind and fell away. Remember this, I remember telling myself, hang on to this. I could feel it all skittering away, whatever conjunction of beauty and improbability I had stumbled upon.

It is hard to describe the indelible bittersweetness of that moment. Which is why, no doubt, it had to be remembered. The very word—*Remember!*—spiraled up like a snake out of a basket, a magic catch in its sound, the doubling of the m—*re mem-memem*—setting up a low murmur full of inchoate associations as if a loved voice were speaking into my ear alone, occultly.

Whether it was the unguarded face of love, or the red gash down the middle of the warring country I was traveling through, or this exhausted farm woman's promise of untold tales that bewitched me, I couldn't say. Over it all rose and remains only the injunction to remember. This, the most impossible command we lay upon ourselves, claimed me and then perversely disappeared, trailing an illusive silken tissue of meaning, without giving a story, refusing to leave me in peace.

*B*ecause everyone "has" a memoir, we all have a stake in how such stories are told. For we do not, after all, simply *have* experience; we are entrusted with it. We must do something—make something—with it. A story, we sense, is the only possible habitation for the burden of our witnessing.

The tantalizing formula of my companion on the Grey-hound—*oh, I could tell you stories*—is the memoirist's opening line, but it has none of the delicious promise of the storyteller's "Once upon a time . . ." In fact, it is a perverse statement. The woman on the bus told me nothing—she fell asleep and escaped to her dreams. For the little sentence inaugurates nothing, and leads nowhere after its *dot dot dot* of expectation. Whatever experience lies tangled within its seductive promise remains forever balled up in the woolly impossibility of telling the-truth-the-whole-truth of a life, any life.

Memoirists, unlike fiction writers, do not really want to "tell a story." They want to tell it *all*—the all of personal experience, of consciousness itself. That includes a story, but also the whole expanding universe of sensation and thought that flows beyond the confines of narrative and proves every life to be not only an isolated story line but a bit of the cosmos, spinning and stream-ing into the great, ungraspable pattern of existence. Memoirists wish to tell their mind, not their story.

The wistfulness implicit in that conditional verb—*I could tell*—conveys an urge more primitive than a storyteller's search for an audience. It betrays not a loneliness for someone who will listen but a hopelessness about language itself and a sad recogni-tion of its limitations. How much reality can subject-verb-object bear on the frail shoulders of the sentence? The sigh within the statement is more like this: I could tell you stories—if only sto-ries could tell what I have in me to tell.

For this reason, autobiographical writing is bedeviled. It is caught in a self which must become a world—and not, please, a narcissistic world. The memoir, once considered a marginal liter-ary form, has emerged in the past decade as the signature genre of the age. "The triumph of memoir is now established fact," James Atlas trumpeted in a cover story on "The Age of the Literary Memoir" in the *New York Times Magazine*. "Fiction," he claimed, "isn't delivering the news. Memoir is."

With its "triumph," the memoir has, of course, not denied the truth and necessity of fiction. In fact, it leans heavily on nov-elistic assumptions. But the contemporary memoir has reaf-firmed the primacy of the first person voice in American imag-inative writing established by Whitman's "Song of Myself." Maybe a reader's love of memoir is less an intrusive lust for con-fession than a hankering for the intimacy of this first-person voice, the deeply satisfying sense of being spoken to privately. More than a story, we want a voice speaking softly, urgently, in our ear. Which is to say, to our heart. That voice carries its implacable command, the ancient murmur that called out to me in the middle of the country in the middle of a war—remem-ber, remember (*I dare you, I tempt you*).

Looking out the Greyhound window that red morning all those years ago, I saw the improbable face of love. But even more puzzling was the cryptic remark of the beloved as she sat next to me. I think of her more often than makes sense. Though he was the beauty, she is the one who comes back. How faint his golden curls have become (he also had a smile, crooked and charming, but I can only remember the idea of it—the image is gone). It is she, stout and unbeautiful, wearing her flowery cotton housedress with a zipper down the middle, who has taken up residence with her canny eye and her accep-tance of adoration. To be loved like that, loved improbably: of course, she had stories to tell. She took it for granted in some unapologetic way, like being born to wealth. Take the money and run.

But that moment before she fell asleep, when she looked pensive, the red morning rising over the Mississippi, was a wistful moment. *I could tell you stories*—but she could not. What she had to tell was too big, too much, too *something,* for her to place in the small shrine that a story is.

When we met—if what happened between us was a meeting—I felt nothing had ever happened to me and nothing ever would. I didn't understand that riding this filthy Greyhound down the middle of bloodied America in the middle of a mutinous war was itself a story and that something *was* happening to me. I thought if something was happening to anybody around me it was happening to people like my boyfriend: They were the heroes, according to the lights that shined for me then. I was just riding shotgun in my own life. I could not have imagined containing, as the farm woman slumped next to me did, the sheer narrative bulk to say, "I could tell you stories," and then drifting off with the secret heaviness of experience into the silence where stories live their real lives, crumbling into the loss we call remembrance.

The boastful little declaration, pathetically conditional (not "I'll tell you a story" but "I could") wavered wistfully for an instant between us. The stranger's remark, launched in the dark of the Greyhound, floated across the human landscape like the lingering tone of a struck bell from a village church, and joined all the silence that ever was, as I turned my face to the window where the world was rushing by along the slow river.

Memory
and
Imagination

When I was seven, my father, who played the violin on Sundays with a nicely tortured flair which we considered artistic, led me by the hand down a long, unlit corridor in St. Luke's School basement, a sort of tunnel that ended in a room full of pianos. There, many little girls and a single sad boy were playing truly tortured scales and arpeggios in a mash of troubled sound. My father gave me over to Sister Olive Marie, who did look remarkably like an olive.

Her oily face gleamed as if it had just been rolled out of a can and laid on the white plate of her broad, spotless wimple. She was a small, plump woman; her body and the small window of her face seemed to interpret the entire alphabet of olive: Her face was a sallow green olive placed upon the jumbo ripe olive of her habit. I trusted her instantly and smiled, glad to have my hand placed in the hand of a woman who made sense, who provided the satisfaction of being what she was: an Olive who looked like an olive.

My father left me to discover the piano with Sister Olive Marie so that one day I would join him in mutually tortured piano-violin duets for the edification of my mother and brother who sat at the table spooning in the last of their pineapple sherbet until their part was called for: They put down their spoons and clapped while we bowed, while the sweet ice in their bowls melted, while the music melted, and we all melted a little into one another for a moment.

But first Sister Olive must do her work. I was shown middle C, which Sister seemed to think terribly important. I stared at middle C, and then glanced away for a second. When my eye returned, middle C was gone, its slim finger lost in the complicated grasp of the keyboard. Sister Olive struck it again, finding it with laughable ease. She emphasized the importance of middle C, its central position, a sort of North Star of sound. I remember thinking, Middle C is the belly button of the piano, an insight whose originality and accuracy stunned me with pride. For the first time in my life I was astonished by metaphor. I hesitated to tell the kindly Olive for some reason; apparently I understood a true metaphor is a risky business, revealing of the self. In fact, I have never, until this moment of writing it down, told my first metaphor to anyone.

Sunlight flooded the room; the pianos, all black, gleamed. Sister Olive, dressed in the colors of the keyboard, gleamed; middle C shimmered with meaning and I resolved never—never—to forget its location: It was the center of the world.

Then Sister Olive, who had had to show me middle C twice but who seemed to have drawn no bad conclusions about me anyway, got up and went to the windows on the opposite wall.

She pulled the shades down, one after the other. The sun was too bright, she said. She sneezed as she stood at the windows with the sun shedding its glare over her. She sneezed and sneezed, crazy little convulsive sneezes, one after another, as helpless as if she had the hiccups.

"The sun makes me sneeze," she said when the fit was over and she was back at the piano. This was odd, too odd to grasp in the mind. I associated sneezing with colds, and colds with rain, fog, snow, and bad weather. The sun, however, had caused Sister Olive to sneeze in this wild way, Sister Olive who gleamed benignly and who was so certain of the location of the center of the world. The universe wobbled a bit and became unreliable. Things were not, after all, necessarily what they seemed. Appearance deceived: Here was the sun acting totally out of character, hurling this woman into sneezes, a woman so mild that she was named, so it seemed, for a bland object on a relish tray.

I was given a red book, the first Thompson book, and told to play the first piece over and over at one of the black pianos where the other children were crashing away. This, I was told, was called practicing. It sounded alluringly adult, practicing. The piece itself consisted mainly of middle C, and I excelled, thrilled by my savvy at being able to locate that central note amidst the cunning camouflage of all the other white keys before me. Thrilled too by the shiny red book that gleamed, as the pianos did, as Sister Olive did, as my eager eyes probably did. I sat at the formidable machine of the piano and got to know middle C intimately, preparing to be as tortured as I could manage one day soon with my father's violin at my side.

But at the moment Mary Katherine Reilly was at my side, playing something at least two or three lessons more sophisticated than my piece. I believe she even struck a chord. I glanced at her from the peasantry of single notes, shy, ready to pay homage.

She turned toward me, stopped playing, and sized me up.

Sized me up and found a person ready to be dominated. Without introduction she said, "My grandfather invented the collapsible opera hat."

I nodded, I acquiesced, I was hers. With that little stroke it was decided between us—that she should be the leader and I the sidekick. My job was admiration. Even when she added, "But he didn't make a penny from it. He didn't have a patent"—even then, I knew and she knew that this was not an admission of powerlessness, but the easy candor of a master, of one who can afford a weakness or two. With the clairvoyance of all fated relationships based on dominance and submission, it was decided in advance: That when the time came for us to play duets, I should always play second piano, that I should spend my allowance to buy her the Twinkies she craved but was not allowed to have, that finally, I should let her copy from my test paper, and when confronted by our teacher, confess with convincing hysteria that it was I, I who had cheated, who had reached above myself to steal what clearly belonged to the rightful heir of the inventor of the collapsible opera hat. . . .

*T*here must be a reason I remember that little story about my first piano lesson. In fact, it isn't a story, just a moment, the beginning of what could perhaps become a story. For the memoirist, more than for the fiction writer, the story seems already *there*, already accomplished and fully achieved in history ("in reality," as we naively say). For the memoirist, the writing of the story is a matter of transcription.

That, anyway, is the myth. But no memoirist writes for long without experiencing an unsettling disbelief about the reliability of memory, a hunch that <u>memory is not, after all, *just* memo-ry</u>. I don't know why I remembered this fragment about my first piano lesson. I don't, for instance, have a single recollection of my first arithmetic lesson, the first time I studied Latin, the first time my grandmother tried to teach me to knit. Yet these things occurred too and must have their stories.

It is the piano lesson that has trudged forward, clearing the haze of forgetfulness, <u>showing itself bright with detail decades after the event</u>. I did not choose to remember the piano lesson. The experience was simply there, like a book that has always been on the shelf, whether I ever read it or not, the binding and title showing as I skim across the contents of my life. On the day I wrote this fragment I happened to take that memory, not some other, from the shelf and paged through it. I found more detail, more event, perhaps a little more entertainment than I had expected, but the memory itself was there from the start. Waiting for me.

[handwritten margin note: details of an adult or a seven-year-old: whose details?]

Wasn't it? When I reread the piano lesson vignette just after I finished it, <u>I realized that I had told a number of lies</u>. I *think* it was my father who took me the first time for my piano lesson, but maybe he only took me to meet my teacher and there was no actual lesson that day. And did I even know then that he played the violin—didn't he take up his violin again much later as a result of my piano playing and not the reverse? And is it even remotely accurate to describe as "tortured" the musicianship of a man who began every day by belting out "Oh What a Beautiful Morning" as he shaved? More: Sister Olive Marie did sneeze in the sun, but was her name Olive? As for her skin tone—I would have sworn it was olivelike. I would have been willing to spend the better part of a morning trying to write the exact description of an imported Italian or Greek olive her face suggested: I wanted to get it right.

But now, were I to write that passage over, it is her intense black eyebrows I would see, for suddenly they seem the central fact of that face, some indicative mark of her serious and patient nature. But the truth is, I don't remember the woman at all. She's a sneeze in the sun and a finger touching middle C.

Worse: I didn't have the Thompson book as my piano text. I'm sure of that because I remember envying children who did have this wonderful book with its pictures of children and animals printed on the pages for music.

As for Mary Katherine Reilly. She didn't even go to grade school with me (and her name isn't Mary Katherine Reilly—but I made that change on purpose). I met her in Girl Scouts and only went to school with her later, in high school. Our relationship was not really one of leader and follower; I played first piano most of the time in duets. She certainly never copied anything from a test paper of mine: She was a better student, and cheating just wasn't a possibility for her. Though her grandfather (or someone in her family) did invent the collapsible opera hat and I remember that she was proud of this fact, she didn't tell me this news as a deft move in a childish power play.

So, what was I doing in this brief memoir? Is it simply an example of the curious relation a fiction writer has to the material of her own life? Maybe. But to tell the truth (if anyone still believes me capable of the truth), I wasn't writing fiction. I was writing memoir—or was trying to. My desire was to be accurate. I wished to embody the myth of memoir: to write as an act of dutiful transcription.

Yet clearly the work of writing a personal narrative caused me to do something very different from transcription. I am forced to admit that memory is not a warehouse of finished stories, not a gallery of framed pictures. I must admit that I invented. But why?

· personal is the key word here

Two whys: Why did I invent and, then, if memory inevitably leads to invention, why do I—why should anybody—write memoir at all?

I must respond to these impertinent questions because they, like the bumper sticker I saw the other day commanding all who read it to QUESTION AUTHORITY, challenge my authority as a memoirist and as a witness.

It still comes as a shock to realize that I don't write about what I know, but in order to find out what I know. Is it possible to convey the enormous degree of blankness, confusion, hunch, and uncertainty lurking in the act of writing? When I am the reader, not the writer, I too fall into the lovely illusion that the words before me which read so inevitably, must also have been written exactly as they appear, rhythm and cadence, language and syntax, the powerful waves of the sentences laying themselves on the smooth beach of the page one after another faultlessly.

But here I sit before a yellow legal pad, and the long page of the preceding two paragraphs is a jumble of crossed-out lines, false starts, confused order. A mess. The mess of my mind trying to find out what it wants to say. This is a writer's frantic, grabby mind, not the poised mind of a reader waiting to be edified or entertained.

I think of the reader as a cat, endlessly fastidious, capable by turns of mordant indifference and riveted attention, luxurious, recumbent, ever poised. Whereas the writer is absolutely a dog, panting and moping, too eager for an affectionate scratch behind the ears, lunging frantically after any old stick thrown in the distance.

The blankness of a new page never fails to intrigue and terrify me. Sometimes, in fact, I think my habit of writing on long yellow sheets comes from an atavistic fear of the writer's stereo-

And/or, does this process take place in people's remembering regardless of whether they write/tell their story or not? ✓

when we write our memories, do we inject ourselves as writers wanting to create memorable writing rather than simply transcribing what ye might see as non-memorable defaults?

typic "blank white page." At least when I begin writing, my page has a wash of color on it, even if the absence of words must finally be faced on a yellow sheet as much as on a blank white one. We all have our ways of whistling in the dark.

If I approach writing from memory with the assumption that I know what I wish to say, I assume that intentionality is running the show. Things are not that simple. Or perhaps writing is even more profoundly simple, more telegraphic and immediate in its choices than the grating wheels and chugging engine of logic and rational intention suppose. The heart, the guardian of intuition with its secret, often fearful intentions, is the boss. Its commands are what a writer obeys—often without knowing it.

This is the beauty of the first draft. And why it's worth pausing a moment to consider what a first draft really is. By my lights, the piano lesson memoir is a first draft. That doesn't mean it exists here exactly as I first wrote it. I like to think I've cleaned it up from the first time I put it down on paper. I've cut some adjectives here, toned down the hyperbole there (though not enough), smoothed a transition, cut a repetition—that sort of housekeeperly tidying up.

But the piece remains a first draft because I haven't yet gotten to know it, haven't given it a chance to tell me anything. For me, writing a first draft is a little like meeting someone for the first time. I come away with a wary acquaintanceship, but the real friendship (if any) is down the road. Intimacy with a piece of writing, as with a person, comes from paying attention to the revelations it is capable of giving, not by imposing my own notions and agenda, no matter how well intentioned they might be.

I try to let pretty much anything happen in a first draft. A careful first draft is a failed first draft. That may be why there are so many inaccuracies in the piano lesson memoir: I didn't censor, I didn't judge, I just kept moving. But I would not publish this piece as a memoir on its own in its present state. It isn't the "lies" in the piece that give me pause, though a reader has a right to expect a memoir to be as accurate as the writer's memory can make it.

The real trouble: The piece hasn't yet found its subject; it isn't yet about what it wants to be about. Note: What *it* wants, not what I want. The difference has to do with the relation a memoirist—any writer—has to unconscious or half-known intentions and impulses in composition.

Now that I have the fragment down on paper, I can read this little piece as a mystery which drops clues to the riddle of my feelings, like a culprit who wishes to be apprehended. My narrative self (the culprit who invented) wishes to be discovered by my reflective self, the self who wants to understand and make sense of a half-remembered moment about a nun sneezing in the sun.

*W*e store in memory only images of value. The value may be lost over the passage of time (I was baffled about why I remembered my sneezing nun), but that's the implacable judgment of feeling: *This,* we say somewhere within us, is something I'm hanging on to. And, of course, often we cleave to things because they possess heavy negative charges. Pain has strong arms.

Over time, the value (the feeling) and the stored memory (the image) may become estranged. Memoir seeks a permanent home for feeling and image, a habitation where they can live together. Naturally, I've had a lot of experiences since I packed away that one from the basement of St. Luke's School; that piano lesson has been effaced by waves of feeling for other moments and episodes. I persist in believing the event has value—after all, I remember it—but in writing the memoir I did not simply relive the experience. Rather, I explored the mysterious relationship between all the images I could round up and the even more impacted feelings that caused me to store the images safely away in memory. Stalking the relationship, seeking the congruence between stored image and hidden emotion—that's the real job of memoir.

By writing about that first piano lesson, I've come to know things I could not know otherwise. But I only know these things as a result of reading this first draft. While I was writing, I was following the images, letting the details fill the room of the page and use the furniture as they wished. I was their dutiful servant—or thought I was. In fact, I was the faithful retainer of my hidden feelings which were giving the commands.

I really did feel, for instance, that Mary Katherine Reilly was far superior to me. She was smarter, funnier, more wonderful in every way—that's how I saw it. Our friendship (or she herself) did not require that I become her vassal, yet perhaps in my heart that was something I sought. I wanted a way to express my admiration. I suppose I waited until this memoir to begin to find the way.

Just as, in the memoir, I finally possess that red Thompson book with the barking dogs and bleating lambs and winsome children. I couldn't (and still can't) remember what my own music book was, so I grabbed the name and image of the one book I could remember. It was only in reviewing the piece after writing it that I saw my inaccuracy. In pondering this "lie," I came to see what I was up to: I was getting what I wanted. Finally.

were these 'false' images created as a child or as an adult? how would this change the meaning? who remembered the 'real' story-adult or child?

The truth of many circumstances and episodes in the past emerges for the memoirist through details (the red music book, the fascination with a nun's name and gleaming face), but these details are not merely information, not flat facts. Such details are not allowed to lounge. They must work. Their labor is the creation of symbol. But it's more accurate to call it the *recognition* of symbol. For meaning is not "attached" to the detail by the memoirist; meaning is revealed. That's why a first draft is important. Just as the first meeting (good or bad) with someone who later becomes the beloved is important and is often reviewed for signals, meanings, omens, and indications.

Now I can look at that music book and see it not only as "a detail" but for what it is, how it acts. See it as the small red door leading straight into the dark room of my childhood longing and disappointment. That red book *becomes* the palpable evidence of that longing. In other words, it becomes symbol. There is no symbol, no life-of-the-spirit in the general or the abstract. Yet a writer wishes—certainly we all wish—to speak about profound matters that are, like it or not, general and abstract. We wish to talk to each other about life and death, about love, despair, loss, and innocence. We sense that in order to live together we must learn to speak of peace, of history, of meaning and values. The big words.

We seek a means of exchange, a language which will renew these ancient concerns and make them wholly, pulsingly ours. Instinctively, we go to our store of private associations for our authority to speak of these weighty issues. We find, in our details and broken, obscured images, the language of symbol. Here memory impulsively reaches out and embraces imagination. That is the resort to invention. It isn't a lie, but an act of necessity, as the innate urge to locate truth always is.

*A*ll right. Invention is inevitable. But why write memoir? Why not call it fiction and be done with it? And if memoir seeks to talk about "the big issues," of history and peace, death and love—why not leave these reflections to those with expert or scholarly knowledge? Why let the common or garden variety memoirist into the club? I'm thinking again of that bumper sticker: Question Authority. Why?

My answer, naturally, is a memoirist's answer. Memoir must be written because each of us must possess a created version of the past. Created: that is, real in the sense of tangible, made of the stuff of a life lived in place and in history. And the downside of any created thing as well: We must live with a version that attaches us to our limitations, to the inevitable subjectivity of our points of view. We must acquiesce to our experience and our gift to transform experience into meaning. You tell me your story, I'll tell you mine.

If we refuse to do the work of creating this personal version of the past, someone else will do it for us. That is the scary political fact. "The struggle of man against power," Milan Kundera's hero in *The Book of Laughter and Forgetting* says, "is the struggle of memory against forgetting." He refers to willful political forgetting, the habit of nations and those in power (Question Authority!) to deny the truth of memory in order to disarm moral and ethical power.

It is an efficient way of controlling masses of people. It doesn't even require much bloodshed, as long as people are entirely willing to give over their personal memories. Whole histories can be rewritten. The books which now seek to deny the existence of the Nazi death camps now fill a room.

What is remembered is what becomes reality. If we "forget"

[Handwritten marginalia, left top:] It is therefore our search for meaning in life. But what is the meaning of life? Why do we need to give it meaning? Does it relate to our lack of fully understanding life or perhaps our lack of something beyond ourselves.

[Handwritten marginalia, left bottom:] This is where 'reporting' truths has become or religion, still creating myths b/c we no longer accept our own myths our Para bless simply b/c they have been factually debunked. But why can't we accept them for the Spiritual guides that they are or have they become outdated?

Auschwitz, if we "forget" My Lai, what then do we remember? And what is the purpose of our remembering? If we think of memory naively, as a simple story, logged like a documentary in the archive of the mind, we miss its beauty but also its function.

The beauty of memory rests in its talent for rendering detail, for paying homage to the senses, its capacity to love the particles of life, the richness and idiosyncrasy of our existence. The function of memory, while experienced as intensely personal, is surprisingly political.

Our capacity to move forward as developing beings rests on a healthy relation with the past. Psychotherapy, that widespread method for promoting mental health, relies heavily on memory and on the ability to retrieve and organize images and events from the personal past. We carry our wounds and perhaps even worse, our capacity to wound, forward with us. If we learn not only to tell our stories but to listen to what our stories tell us— to write the first draft and then return for the second draft—we are doing the work of memory.

Memoir is the intersection of narration and reflection, of storytelling and essay writing. It can present its story *and* consider the meaning of the story. The first commandment of fiction— Show, Don't Tell—is not part of the memoirist's faith. Memoirists must show *and* tell. Memoir is a peculiarly open form, inviting broken and incomplete images, half-recollected fragments, all the mass (and mess) of detail. It offers to shape this confusion—and, in shaping, of course, it necessarily creates a work of art, not a legal document. But then, even legal documents are only valiant attempts to consign the truth, the whole truth, and nothing but the truth to paper. Even they remain versions.

Locating touchstones—the red music book, the olive Olive, my father's violin playing—is satisfying. Who knows why?

Perhaps we all sense that we can't grasp the whole truth and nothing but the truth of our experience. Just can't be done.

What can be achieved, however, is a version of its swirling, changing wholeness. A memoirist must acquiesce to selectivity, like any artist. The version we dare to write is the only truth, the only relationship we can have with the past. Refuse to write your life and you have no life. That is the stern view of the memoirist.

Personal history, logged in memory, is a sort of slide projector flashing images on the wall of the mind. And there's precious little order to the slides in the rotating carousel. Beyond that confusion, who knows who is running the projector? A memoirist steps into this darkened room of flashing, unorganized images and stands blinking for a while. Maybe for a long while. But eventually, as with any attempt to tell a story, it is necessary to put something first, then something else. And so on, to the end. That's a first draft. Not necessarily the truth, not even *a* truth sometimes, but the first attempt to create a shape.

The first thing I usually notice at this stage of composition is the appalling inaccuracy of the piece. Witness my first piano lesson draft. Invention is screamingly evident in what I intended to be transcription. But here's the further truth: I feel no shame. In fact, it's only now that my interest in the piece quickens. For I can see what isn't there, what is shyly hugging the walls, hoping not to be seen. I see the filmy shape of the next draft. I see a more acute version of the episode or—this is more likely—an entirely new piece rising from the ashes of the first attempt.

The next draft of the piece would have to be true re-vision, a new seeing of the materials of the first draft. Nothing merely cosmetic will do—no rouge buffing up the opening sentence, no glossy adjective to lift a sagging line, nothing to attempt covering a patch of gray writing.

I can't say for sure, but my hunch is the revision would lead me to more writing about my father (Why was I so impressed by that ancestral inventor of the collapsible opera hat? Did I feel I had nothing as remarkable in my own background?). I begin to think perhaps Sister Olive is less central to this business than she appears to be. She is meant to be a moment, not a character. I'm probably wasting my time on her, writing and writing around her in tight descriptive circles, waiting for the real subject to reveal itself. My father!

So I might proceed, if I were to undertake a new draft of the memoir. I begin to feel a relationship developing between a former self and me.

And even more important, a relationship between an old world and me. Some people think of autobiographical writing as the precious occupation of the unusually self-absorbed. Couldn't the same accusation be hurled at a lyric poet, at a novelist—at anyone with the audacity to present a personal point of view? True memoir is written, like all literature, in an attempt to find not only a self but a world.

The self-absorption that seems to be the impetus and embarrassment of autobiography turns into (or perhaps always was) a hunger for the world. Actually, it begins as hunger for *a* world, one gone or lost, effaced by time or a more sudden brutality. But in the act of remembering, the personal environment expands, resonates beyond itself, beyond its "subject," into the endless and tragic recollection that is history. We look at old family photographs in which we stand next to black, boxy Fords, and are wearing period costumes, and we do not gaze fascinated because there we are young again, or there we are standing, as we never will again in life, next to our mother. We stare and drift because there we are historical. It is the dress, the black car that dazzle us now and draw us beyond our mother's bright arms which once caught us. We reach into the attractive impersonality of something more significant than ourselves. We write memoir, in other words. We accept the humble position of writing a version, the consolation prize for our acknowledgment we cannot win "the whole truth and nothing but."

I suppose I write memoir because of the radiance of the past—it draws me back and back to it. Not that the past is beautiful. In our communal memoir, in history, the darkness we sense is not only the dark of forgetfulness. The darkness is history's tunnel of horrors with its tableaux vivants of devastation. The blasted villages, the hunted innocents, the casual acquiescence to the death camps and tiger cages are back there in the fetid holes of history.

But still, the past is radiant. It sheds the light of lived life. One who writes memoir wishes to step into that light, not to see one's own face—that is not possible—but to feel the length of shadow cast by the light. No one owns the past, though typically the first act of new political regimes, whether of the left or the right, is an attempt to rewrite history, to grab the past and make it over so the end comes out right. So their power looks inevitable.

No one owns the past, but it is a grave error (another age would have said a grave sin) not to inhabit memory. Sometimes I think it is all we really have. But that may be melodrama, the bad habit of the memoirist, coming out. At any rate, memory possesses authority for the fearful self in a world where it is necessary to claim authority in order to Question Authority.

There may be no more pressing intellectual need in our culture than for people to become sophisticated about the function of memory. The political implications of the loss of memory are obvious. The authority of memory is a personal confirmation of selfhood, and therefore the first step toward ethical development.

I'd like to think more deeply about the politics of memory. Is it the loss of memory of the acceptance of others creating memories for us that is more dangerous—just so much the recreation of the past but the creation of tomorrow's memories

To write one's life is to live it twice, and the second living is both spiritual and historical, for a memoir reaches deep within the personality as it seeks its narrative form and it also grasps the life-of-the-times as no political analysis can.

Our most ancient metaphor says life is a journey. Memoir is travel writing, then, notes taken along the way, telling how things looked and what thoughts occurred. Show *and* tell. But I cannot think of the memoirist as a tourist. The memoir is no guide book. This traveler lives the journey idiosyncratically, taking on mountains, enduring deserts, marveling at the lush green places. Moving through it all faithfully, not so much a survivor with a harrowing tale to tell as that older sort of traveler, the pilgrim, seeking, wondering.

· Differences between journaling and writing memoir — one living in the present, recording feelings and thoughts, the other living in the past (?) Would a Buddhist write memoir?

Does writing or reading memoir make us more aware of the present? Or, is it our inability to let go of the past? ← ATTACHMENT?

WHAT ARE OUR ATTACHMENTS IN writing MEMOIR (or anything for that matter)? A need for permanence? perhaps an exercise in letting go (seems unlikely)? A need for acceptance? Or, creation? This latter I can accept as a Buddhist. So, how will this change my practice?

The *Mayflower* Moment: Reading Whitman during the Vietnam War

In 1968, believe it or not, you blushed when you asked your doctor for birth control pills. Twenty-two and unmarried, wearing the stiff paper garment which, about that time, doctors began to issue for examinations in place of crisply laundered cotton gowns. Cheaper, no doubt, although the nurse, starchy herself, said, "More sanitary." Every change was an improvement: I didn't pause over the nineteenth-century assumption of progress as I reached out for the twentieth-century solution to my problems.

Lying there on the table, my feet in the stirrups, waiting for the doctor to come in, I wondered briefly if this change in exam gowns had put someone out of a job: Economics were strangely powerful, though I rarely considered the subject. I was arty, as my brother, a dentistry student, often said.

Then the doctor was in the room, and I moved on to the small but keen humiliation of asking for the key to personal freedom from a man wearing a $500 suit while I was dressed in a large blue Kleenex. He was a nice man. At a previous visit he had been bald as a cue ball; this time his head was a riot of dark curls. A toupee. The vanity was somehow reassuring. It made him more like me, more feminine, someone who understood the gloss we must put on reality to get through. He handed over the pills as easily as if I'd asked for Life Savers (ah, I had).

A doctor like this was so nice maybe you found yourself saying you were getting married—"next summer"—so he would not think evil thoughts about you, or simply refuse to give you a prescription. Don't go to a Catholic doctor! we warned each other. Or maybe you didn't say you were getting married because you had rehearsed the scene heavily the night before with your girlfriends (as you still, though not for long, called them): *You* were not going to lie. You were going to march right in there and *tell* the doctor to give you the goods.

And I did, sort of. Then I blushed.

That's how it was. Afterward, I went across the street to the Brothers Delicatessen in downtown Minneapolis and ordered a Reuben sandwich ("Big Enough to Feed Two!"), a piece of five-layer chocolate cake, a pot of tea, and a glass of water. The glass of water was business; the rest was glee.

I put my purse beside me, along with the book I was carrying. I held the plastic circle in my hand. Enlightenment welled up in me, the hilarity of revelation: It's so *simple*. The little pill—I marveled at its tininess, I bowed to medical science—popped, eagerly it seemed, out of its Day 1 slot. Imitating this exuberance, I popped Day 1 lightly into my mouth, took a swallow of water, and let technology have its way with me. Today is the first day of the rest of your life, right?

I settled into the Reuben sandwich which, though big enough for two, was going to feed just one and no doubt about it now. I picked up the book (always bring a book to the doctor's office; they always make you wait: the wisdom of my mother—who didn't know about *this* doctor's appointment). I propped the book between the sugar dispenser and the plate, and I read and ate and was happy in my new high-tech body.

The book was the Modern Library edition of *Leaves of Grass.* I had just taken care of personal life neatly. Now I moved on to America which, at the time, seemed to present more unsettling troubles even than sex did. But where was the pill for that?

[handwritten: Use of pause allows reader to settle in situation himself]

The idea of America. The idea of friendship as a model for sexual relations and for citizenship. The very idea of ideas, the allure of speculation, the satisfaction of considering the Big Questions, of mapping things out. And always, the reassuring (because I was just beginning to write) elevation of the role of the "poet and literatus." These, for me, were Whitman's initial appeal.

It seems now as if I read Whitman all that year and the next two, 1969 and 1970; it seems as if I read no one but Whitman. Or perhaps I read others as footnotes or responses to the main text which was always his.

For this was also the time when I began to read contemporary American poetry. The poets I read then will probably always people my private roster of our national poetry, and the ones I happened not to read then are figures I sketched in later; they are ghosts with no power to spook me. I didn't happen to read Robert Lowell then, except for a few anthology pieces, and so, although I've been instructed to understand that he is more

[handwritten, left margin: Use of a classic American writer]

important than, say, Louis Simpson, it doesn't work. I was read-ing Simpson's *At the End of the Open Road* in 1968, neatly writ-ing "image," "surrealism," "metaphor," "irony" next to particular lines, as if reverent labeling would assure me a place in the king-dom. I wanted to be a poet too.

I read with the hunger of my Victorian novel reading in high school. It was a second childhood of mesmerized reading, only this time the books were modern, minimal, and austere even in their physical aspect: the lean volumes of living poets. It was easy to carry ten of them home from the library at a crack. And—ominous good luck which I rued later when my own first book of poems was published—nobody else seemed to be checking out these skinny books, so I always had my pick.

I was consoled by these contemporary poets not simply because their world view mirrored my own less articulate, form-less one. In fact, as feminism claimed more territory, my heroes sometimes disappointed me—though I noted Whitman's good habit of writing "men and women," rather than just "men."

The consolation these poets provided may seem at first abstract, barely recognizable as passion. Yet it was fiercely pas-sionate: I loved Whitman and the poets I saw as his heirs because they addressed the question of "a national self." They pondered the American identity—did it exist? What was it? Would such an identity help the individual citizen?

Asking the "right" questions

It was the Vietnam War era. Like a lot of people, I felt des-perate about being an American, an identity which until then had seemed attractive and had been associated in my mind (as poetry itself was) with a radiant goodness given to large-spirited gestures. At the Brothers Delicatessen I had swallowed the lozenge of personal revolution. I was an earnest communicant—at last—at the modern altar after long tarrying in the vestibule of Catholic girlhood. But all was not well. I waited for "experi-

grounding the story in the "real" the personal makes it ~~seem~~ believable.

ence" to claim me, for "personal life" to happen—and I was ready. Nothing bad can happen to me, I truly thought. The pill instantly became metaphorical and represented not only freedom but safety.

But I was already nursing a broken heart. And nothing had even happened to me yet. I felt jilted by the nation. As I looked at the evening news, it seemed I didn't *know* my own people. They were alien. Only "they" weren't conveniently foreign: They were we. This alienation fired itself into an overpowering desire to analyze the American self.

As far as I could tell, "the national self" had either never existed or, if it had, was now grotesquely ravaged by our role in Vietnam. I did not feel American. Or rather, I felt terribly, grievously American, but I didn't know what to do about it or what that meant. I registered shame as a national emotion. And I felt a powerful sense of having been cheated. But mainly I was confused. Who were we, anyway?

I felt I knew who I was: a modern woman with a body that ticked now not like a bomb planted in a locker but like a tightly wound porcelain clock painted with flowers, as feminine as you please but also, since my trip to the gynecologist, a reliable machine.

But I didn't know who *we* were. And that drove me, as it did many others, to fervent analysis, looking for explanations and discussions of the American self. Beyond my protest of the war, I was impelled by a need to consider the larger issue of the national identity, much as a woman who goes into therapy because her marriage is on the rocks and she's unable to eat solid food or brush her teeth without weeping. She ends up settling the "presenting problem," and staying in her huddle to unravel a much denser skein of yarn going back to childhood and to the chancy cards dealt at birth: the fact of being a woman, or a

Catholic, or a Jew. In this case, the immediate anguish over the Vietnam War led to the conundrum of being an American.

Beyond my personal ambition and desire to be a poet, I trusted poetry. I had always known I wanted to write, but I had assumed I would be a reporter or some kind of journalist. I hadn't considered "being a poet," although I had always written poems. In a confused way, I thought being a poet was a posthumous occupation: People decided after you were dead if you'd been one. But I turned to poetry in a more complete way at this time, as reader and as a young writer, because it was one of the places I recognized American voices speaking with candor.

It was a time when, like so many of my generation, I trusted little I read or heard. That may be why I have the sense that I read poetry for consolation. Also for the news, even though it was usually bad news. But at least the poets I was reading or whom I heard at the antiwar readings (Kinnell, Bly, Snyder, Wright, Levertov, to name a few) were able to indicate a relation between the current national trauma and the past. "Folks expect of the poet to indicate . . . the path between reality and their souls," Whitman wrote in the preface to the 1855 edition of *Leaves of Grass*. "Men and women perceive beauty well enough . . . probably as well as he." I believed that, and did not read poetry for an aesthetic rush. I looked for "the path" in the poets I read.

These contemporary poets had a sense of the national self, an ethical and psychological instinct, which radical political commentators, with whom I basically agreed, often lacked. As for the mainstream press and our elected leaders—we were choking on their lies, their subterfuge and cowardice. It is so much accepted now as part of the national relation to that era that "Vietnam was a mistake" that it is hard to recapture the anguish and loneliness many people felt as they protested not only against the war but against people and institutions they would otherwise have trusted. I recognized in contemporary poetry a voice, quite a few voices, I could trust. I cannot think of Whitman without thinking of these contemporary poets. They are part of the same book I was trying then to read: the story of the self in the nation.

Louis Simpson said the open road led to the used car lot, and I was not only shocked but subtly thrilled, as if I'd arrived at the denouement of a compelling story begun in Whitman's dream of the American journey. James Wright said he could not bear

> *to allow my poor brother my body to die*
> *In Minneapolis.*
> *The old man Walt Whitman our countryman*
> *Is now in America our country*
> *Dead.*
>
> *But he was not buried in Minneapolis*
> *At least.*
> *And no more may I be*
> *Please God.*

Minneapolis—not, for me, the name of a flyover city, but Minneapolis *where I lived*. I shivered the provincial shiver, the unfamiliar glamour of significance. It hardly mattered that in the poem my town was the metaphor for everything crummy and worthless: Our name was on the paper, we were part of the story, in direct (if negative) relation to Whitman himself. Maybe the end of the open road was Minneapolis. I was in place.

These poems were new at the time, and I took them personally, which is the only way to take poetry, to know something *is* poetry. I was dazzled by the ferocious disappointment of these poets of the generation immediately preceding my own. I took in their disillusion in heavy drafts at the same time that I was reading Whitman's theoretical rhapsodies, especially in his preface to the 1855 edition and the long essay, "Democratic Vistas."

I felt, reading these contemporary poets, like a sneak who turns to the last page of a thriller but who still goes diligently back to find out how the puzzling crime began. For me, Whitman was the beginning. He was there along with Emily Dickinson. I liked the idea that our literary history—my version—began with these two poised above us like an icon of sexual equality, proof of an evenhanded distribution of genius. Two odd ducks, she with her spectral virginity and brief, rectitudinous metric lines, acute and strange; and he cramming the page with his radically long lines, practically jabbering at times, transfiguring his sexuality, which bewildered him, into a vision of democracy—"the dear love of comrades." I was entirely satisfied with Mother and Father, eccentric as they were.

But I chose Father, as girls often do. I would have become a Whitmanian, had it been possible, the way Russians once became Tolstoyans. Whitman advised against this sort of thing:

> *Are you the new person drawn toward me?*
> *To begin with take warning, I am surely far different from what*
> *   you suppose;*
> *Do you suppose you will find in me your ideal?*
> *Do you think it so easy to have me become your lover?*
> *Do you think the friendship of me would be unalloy'd*
> *   satisfaction?*
> *Do you think I am trusty and faithful?*
> *Do you see no further than this facade, this smooth and*
> *   tolerant manner of me?*

I paid no heed. I suppose I wanted to find a gorgeously optimistic voice to reassure me that, in spite of the evidence (those human ears dangling from the string on a GI's belt in a *Life* magazine picture), the national self could be saved, that my life—just beginning as I felt—would not be indentured to the guilt of appalling crimes, but would continue to tick along in its flower-painted clock, as free in spirit as my toupee-wearing gynecologist had made me in body.

I clung to Whitman because he had a theoretical bent, which I read as entirely sunny: He was not the poet of death and lilacs for me, but the man who said things like, "Of all nations the United States with veins full of poetical stuff most need poets and will doubtless have the greatest and use them the greatest."

He said we were a spiritual and poetic people. On the other hand, I read Bly and Wright, Kinnell and Levertov because they expressed the immediate horror and grief; they kept the moral pulse beating. I read them and I read Whitman in a balancing act: bad news, good news.

But I was glad Whitman's book was fat, endless as an ancient sacred text, and that these others were thin, modest modern footnotes to scripture. The contemporary verdict was grave, but these living poets also turned to Whitman for the prophetic gleam. Reading him was like touching base. For in Whitman, the national self—what he called "the American stock personality"—held its head high and looked out at the world guilelessly, like the poetic self he said we were meant to be.

*I*t made a great difference to me that Whitman wrote prose as well as poetry; it actually heightened his authority as a poet. The poetry and the essays, taken together (and I did take them together), made him a bard. He sang—but he also speculated, prophesied, admonished.

The prose also made him more accessible, gave range and intimacy to anything he touched. I wanted to be a writer, and the times I was living in drew me more deeply into poetry than I had expected. I had just graduated from the university and had started my first job, working the night desk at the *St. Paul Pioneer Press.* Maybe it was natural that I felt especially kindred to a poet who, like me, had been a working journalist and to whom prose was not an alien genre but another way of speaking.

Whitman might sing of love in his poems, but he also thought about it, speculated about it, in his essays. My favorite of his love poems, my single favorite of his short lyrics, was this one from the "Children of Adam" section of *Leaves*:

> *I heard you solemn-sweet pipes of the organ as last Sunday morn I*
> *   pass'd the church,*
> *Winds of autumn, as I walk'd the woods at dusk I heard your long-*
> *   stretch'd sighs up above so mournful,*
> *I heard the perfect Italian tenor singing at the opera, I heard the*
> *   soprano in the midst of the quartet singing;*
> *Heart of my love! you too I heard murmuring low through one of*
> *   the wrists around my head,*
> *Heard the pulse of you when all was still ringing little bells last*
> *   night under my ear.*

examples

I moved easily from this sheer lyric grace with its erotic lucidity to his speculations in the essays about "the dear love of comrades," which he proposed as the basis of a genuine American democracy. We weren't going to be a nation based on hierarchy as the old feudal world had been; we were not even going to settle for the correct comfort of being a nation of laws.

We were going to be pals, a nation of buddies. This vision delighted me.

For one thing, it was warm and attractive: I was glad of the family feeling. As it was, my own family and I were enacting the classic Vietnam-era battles and arguments, ornamented in our baroque Catholic way where hierarchy was the whole point. Sometimes I wasn't sure whether my father and I were fighting about the war, my boyfriend's long hair, my long hair, the smoking of marijuana by me or by "the nation's youth" ("Do you want to become an *addict?* Your brother says it could lead to addiction." My brother, the dentistry student, possessed the authority of science; I worked for the newspaper and was arty. I could never win an argument).

All the arguments in our family, in everybody's family, seemed to lead to or from Vietnam and yet Vietnam was not the entire point. The desire for personal identification with a larger-than-self heritage was the point. In "Democratic Vistas" Whitman said, "democracy . . . ever seeks to bind all nations, all men into a brotherhood, a family." I wanted to believe this—as an American, but also as the troubled and troublesome (I started the dinner table arguments) member of a real family.

One Sunday, while my father was changing a light bulb in the dining room chandelier, standing on top of the very table we fought across, I announced I wasn't going to Mass anymore, ever. Period. He said nothing, just continued screwing in the new light bulb, looming above me, as powerfully mysterious as an electrical charge, no matter what rebellion I visited upon him with my gnatlike persistence, my protests, and arch refusals and ardent avowals.

So. I didn't belong to the Church. Nor to a happy family. And I didn't stand up for the national anthem at ball games. The only thing I belonged to was my generation—hardly a permanent address, although I tried to make it home for a long time. But reading Whitman I belonged: to what I felt was the true nation, to those who lived in the magic of the possible, in mourning for America, the pure idea.

Here, in Whitman, America shimmered for me in its refracted identity, the only truly innocent identity it has ever had: America the idea. As Whitman put it,

> . . . the true nationality of the States, the genuine union, when we come to a mortal crisis, is, and is to be, after all, neither the written law, nor (as generally supposed,) either self-interest, or common pecuniary or material objects—but the fervid and tremendous IDEA. . . .

I could dream the American idea over again with Whitman even though air-conditioned, transistor radio-equipped American helicopters were dropping napalm on green villages at that very moment. I could escape American history which was a bad dream and enter the dream of America which I wished could be history. A sleight of hand, a last-ditch attempt to return to the purity of abstraction, to the *Mayflower* moment, the radiant arrival in paradise before anything had happened. Ourselves— but rinsed of history. Whitman, as I read him, was an invitation to innocence. (we never had)

If the gospel means "good news," I read Whitman as gospel. He had had his war, calamitous and divisive of the national self, and now we were having ours. He had his aberrant sexuality and we (American women) had our sudden "sexual liberation."

Out of the ashes of the Civil War and out of his ambivalence about his own sexuality, Whitman fashioned his thrilling American conception, fusing together sex and citizenship, envisioning a country full of charmed lovers with arms around each others' waists. Our relation as a nation would be chosen and free, affectionate and "adhesive," as he put it. The sad American patrimony, the inheritance of alienation under the mantle of individualism, was, in Whitman's vision, transfigured into a rich and radiant ideal of nationhood.

If, after his war, Whitman could dream such a dream, why couldn't we? We weren't the first American generation saddled with disillusion and rancor. I forgot, of course, that Whitman felt his war had been won, and disaster averted. I'm not sure, even now, that any victory, any sense of transcendence, was possible for my generation once Vietnam became our crucible. When the war finally ended in 1975 (it did end, didn't it?), there was a curious lack of joy. No dancing in Times Square, no elation. The word wasn't "Peace," but the lackluster phrase, "The troops pulled out." We hadn't won; we hadn't even lost. It was just over—sort of. All that was left was to write the books.

pause

*F*or most nations a heritage is a sort of goulash of history and legend and shared values. In our case, it seemed, history was bypassed, replaced by the utopic reliance on the future. "America," Whitman writes at the beginning of "Democratic Vistas,"

counts, as I reckon, for her justification and success (for who, as yet, dare claim success?) almost entirely on the future. Nor is that hope unwarranted. Today, ahead, though dimly yet, we see, in vistas, a copious, sane, gigantic offspring. For our New World I consider far less important for what it has done, or what it is, than for results to come. Sole among nationalities, these States have assumed the task to put in forms of lasting power and practicality, on areas of amplitude rivaling the operations of the physical kosmos, the moral political spec- ulations of ages, long, long deferr'd, the democratic republi- can principle, and the theory of development and perfection by voluntary standards, and self-reliance.

I read Whitman ahistorically, as if "Democratic Vistas" had not been written in 1871, but in 1971. The dream was alive, the idea was possible—it all lay ahead, it was all in the future. Here I was, one hundred years later, two world wars into history, bored by the stale pioneer imagery of the country (The New Frontier, the "frontiers of space"), not recognizing that the boredom masked yet another shame, the plain fact of massacre which is the underbelly of the pioneer spirit, of "settling the country." Settling the country, pacifying the village: the cooing language we use for our rough stuff.

I wanted, in a self-righteous way as well as helplessly, the only American birthright I could imagine: to step off the *Mayflower* onto undefiled land, unlimited possibility, unwritten history. And to believe, as I put my foot down, that glorious, pure ideas would be the controlling influence in this world.

I suppose I was truly American in this desire, and entirely conceptual: I was propelled and consoled by the *idea* of America. I thought I was seeking—and finding in Whitman—a national identity. But I was looking for something else. I wanted to find America innocent. And as a woman very purposefully equipping my body for "experience," I secretly wished to remain inno- cent, cerebral, untouched.

Innocence was the only "national self" I was prepared to acknowledge and pledge allegiance to. Whitman provided that— or my reading of him did. We might be untrue to this self—as the poets at the antiwar readings reminded us—but at least the

[margin handwritten note: Idealist but also slightly delusional.]

self existed. I think Whitman saved me from a paralyzing self-hatred. He fixed my mind on a vision. But innocence, once it can be named as such, is about the past. I was nostalgic before I even got started. I thought, reading Whitman, I had a spiritual awakening. But it was rude awakenings that lay ahead.

My best friend's husband went to prison as a draft resister in the late sixties. Then, in 1970, the man I lived with went too, having bewildered his Illinois draft board with a letter that explained that because Walt Whitman had said, "Dismiss whatever insults your own soul," he was dismissing his draft card (see enclosed, etc., etc.).

This struck me as heroic, Whitmanian, independent: the action of a patriot. I am still loyal to that act, even though at the time I was more taken by the romance of it than by the morality. The slow, annoyingly dull details of courts and incarceration blunted the dagger of the initial gesture. What about dismissing the judge, the prison, the war itself, the whole rotting carcass of imperialism? Didn't they insult the soul too?

At the trial I was dismayed to realize that, unlike a courtroom scene on Perry Mason, it was impossible from the visitors' gallery to hear a single thing either judge or defendant was saying. The grand dismissal was a mumble, and then my patriot was in handcuffs and leg irons, and the whole thing was over.

One dismissal made for a raft of acceptances, for suddenly the body, unlike the soul, could not do much dismissing. My God, I thought as they led him away, they're really going to put him in *prison*.

What else, honey? a small sage voice within said. My focus on the ideal hadn't allowed me a peephole on reality, as if prison had never been a possibility, when in fact it had always been the only possible result of that moment when, together, we had stood on the corner of an elm-lined street in our midwestern university town, I opening the mouth of the blue mailbox, he dropping the envelope into the dark hole.

The beautiful directive had been followed: An insult to the soul had been dismissed. But I think for many people who made such decisions, who responded to the Whitmanian vision, or who were affected by the decisions of others close to them, the real lesson and effect came later. For it turned out that the initial dismissal caused one to live in an environment (either in prison or in the reflected life of acts with consequences) where insulting things could not be dismissed. The first dismissal was important—because it was a genuine act, one with consequences. But the acceptances that followed were the crucible of character.

For it is in those things which cannot be dismissed or chosen, which are not conceptual or ideal, but which must be acquiesced to and assimilated that "identity" of self or of nation begins to achieve authenticity. Not from the *Mayflower* to the American paradise, but from the bluffs of the buffalo hunt to the reservation is the journey toward American truth.

Vision is necessary—and our literature is rich with the power of dream. But there must be a moment when one is no longer just stepping ashore onto the unmarked New World, eyelashes aflutter like an ingenue at a first dance, waiting for something to happen, something wonderful, something imagined. The future is here, now, and the past is full of actual deeds, real history. Utopias hardly have the meat on their bones to sustain a people in grave times.

I saw a number of letters that young men sent to their draft boards during those years. Whitman was quoted frequently, only a shade less often than Thoreau: "Dismiss whatever insults your own soul." "The soul has that measureless pride which consists in never acknowledging any lessons but its own." But it was acting on the vision, taking the utopic idea seriously into history, and then living with the consequences, which finally gave the idea dignity—or not.

Many of the young men who went to prison felt they ruined their lives. Their wives left them or they found themselves mired in terrible depressions, even (or especially) when they got out of prison, nursing dark nights of the soul and growing fatally ironic about their own grand gestures. All of a sudden there was nothing left to dismiss; they could only endure. Hanging in there lacks the élan of dismissing whatever insults your own soul. I wonder how many of those young men—not young anymore—ended up dismissing Whitman or dismissing themselves, or simply hating the tender idealism which they took with them into prison.

Recently at a party I overheard a conversation between an ex-draft resister and a woman who said to him, "Well, I suppose you feel pretty good about how you handled yourself during the war. I mean, you were right."

He laughed. "Oh, I just had to prove I was a hero. It really got my father's attention." Said without rancor. He seemed amused with himself. There was a long-ago-and-faraway quality to his relation with his own protest. The woman was a little put off, and did not like his lightness. The self-mockery was gentle, but maybe she had never dismissed what had insulted her own soul and didn't know how foolish that makes you feel.

Foolish and full to the brim with contradictions, as Whitman knew. The test of dismissing whatever insults your own soul turned out to be the ability to hold in balance all the foolishness and contradictions that followed in the wake of a gesture which was both ideal and very real.

*A*nd then there was the fact of charm. Whitman charmed me. Charm is powerful in normal human relations, in conversation, for instance, where being boorishly right is *merely* being right. Oddly enough, charmlessness is not only a form of aggression but of dishonesty, a revocation of an essential part of the candor that lies at the heart of respect for others. For in human relations to dispense with charm is to dispense with the other person.

To speak, to write, without charm is to make utterances without reference to a reality outside oneself. It is an act devoid of the playfulness of art, without the attractive humility of one who knows absolutely that others exist and therefore feels drawn to please them, because to give them an instant of pleasure is to acknowledge their existence. And if Whitman often admonished, it is a mark of his genius that he managed to charm, even as he struck close to the bone.

I might snort when I read Whitman carrying on—his "America *ma femme!*" or his "man-balls and man-root." But he gave me a relish for nerviness in language, for declaration and a personal renaming of even the simplest facts of existence which I value still.

Even a contorted phrase like "the perennial health-action of the air we call the weather" charmed me—not because it was beautiful ("No one will get at my verses who insists upon viewing them as a literary performance, or attempt at such performance, or as aiming toward art of aestheticism"), but because such lines attested to Whitman's personal inspection of the universe, down to the last detail. The first rule was to take nothing for granted; the second rule was, however, to *take* everything, like a primitive photographer with the world's first camera. "Who knows the curious mystery of the eyesight?"

Whitman's greed appealed to me too. "I contain multitudes." On the other side of that statement was the irrepressible avidity that was crying, More, more! I loved his catalogs partly for the serenity to be found in any litany; there is something religious about a list. But also I loved them for the proprietary, house-keeperly tabulation: He was counting up the national silver, listing rivers, toting up the states, nationalities, regions, fields, and forests. It was another, more concrete, way of stalking the national identity. Our features went on and on; we had a shape, we could be named.

As a reader I was charmed to be addressed directly ("dear, earnest reader"), to be appealed to:

> . . . the reader is to do something for himself, must be on the alert, must himself or herself construct indeed the poem, argument, history, metaphysical essay—the text furnishing the hints, the clue, the start or frame-work. Not the book needs so much to be complete thing, but the reader of the book does.

He even flirted:

Camerado, this is no book,
Who touches this touches a man,
(Is it night? Are we here together alone?)

He gave instructions about where to read his book (outside, if possible, under a tree), he practically cozied up on the reader's lap. Is there anyone who has insisted so strenuously that he *is* his book and who has as nearly accomplished that magic trick? The real camerado he succeeded joining his life with was his book.

No wonder there is, then, "the book," not many books. The self, if it is healthy, does not divide but contains its multitudes, its contradictions within easy grasp and range. Whitman, paradoxically then, who is often cited as the source of the loose, even sloppy, American poetic diction, is, in fact, the father of immaculate form: everything fits. Another of his contradictions. Another charm.

*B*y 1973 I wasn't reading Whitman anymore. I wasn't taking the pill either. Technology had let me down. There were ominous "findings" about blood clots and other side effects from "long-term reliance on the pill as a form of contraception." Long-term reliance! I'd planned to pop those little numbers till kingdom come. Then my mother got breast cancer (she recovered) and my nice gynecologist thought it best "in your case, given the high risk situation" that I "discontinue use."

He suggested an IUD. But my honeymoon with modern science was over. The pill had been pristine and almost abstract, a metaphor from Day 1. But this other gadget looked like a pop tab from a can of Pepsi. Later, one of my friends, rendered infertile by an IUD, financed her graduate school education with a court settlement she made with the Dalkon Shield people.

I moved on to the diaphragm. I tried to be cheerful about it, but that old contraceptive magic was gone. The pill had leapt out of its little slot eagerly, but the diaphragm, lathered correctly with its goo, had a habit of springing madly, perversely, out of my hand, across the room, behind the radiator where, when I retrieved it, it was covered with a soft fur of dust like a mushroom feathered with mold. When someone told me that the diaphragm had been invented in 1890, I felt the humiliation was complete—back to the nineteenth century with us. We hadn't even had the vote then.

I had stopped reading Whitman. Personal life, sexual life certainly, could not be so easily regulated as I had thought in 1968. My friends and my boyfriend were out of prison, but the war still went on. I didn't believe anymore—how could I?—that a national self, no matter how deeply desired (and I still felt the desire), could be chosen or synthesized by an act of will. Not even by an act of the imagination.

America was not an idea, not anymore. It was not a matter of the future. We had not all arrived on the *Mayflower,* blinking at the New World's brightness, grasping an irreproachable Idea. There had been slave ships and steerage passages too. Soon there would be "boat people," as if the most recent arrivals were named for us and were not emblematic of their Asian history but of our own: Americans as eternal new arrivals, forever disembarking. America refused to·be an idea. It was a country, and its national self—that personality Whitman tried so valiantly to identify—was emerging as national identity always does: out of history, out of circumstance and experience.

I had leaned too hard on Whitman, had not read his contradictions into him though I'd paid lip service to all of that. I had gone to him for a package deal, for the pill. He even looked like a guru—he looked like Tolstoy.

I don't blame myself. He certainly had his "dear, earnest reader" in me, and he wouldn't be interested in apologies. What can you do? We all contain multitudes, not just Whitman.

But I realize, as I go through my old Modern Library edition of *Leaves of Grass* (how soft the pages are from use, how frequent my underlinings, how diligent the margin notes where I indicated "the roles of the poet," "the democratic ideal"), in this rereading, I see how much Whitman has mattered to me in ways I hadn't been aware of.

"It's so *simple!*" I find myself saying, a frail echo of that ~~thread~~ enlightened glee at the Brothers Delicatessen—Whitman matters because he made *himself* a book. The magic, the genius, is that although he says he sings himself, that he is a "kosmos," even so these assertions are the opposite, in fact the denial, of self-aggrandizement. In my earlier reading, I always saw his cheer, his invitation, his constant insistence on relation. Now I see his vast privacy. His invitation was really to my own self, my own book. And that was the secret power of his attraction for me, secret even to me.

I would not even be writing this today in the way I am—as a memoir—if Whitman had not written "Song of Myself," if he had not done that astonishing thing: pose for his own portrait and call it America.

He placed himself between the personal and the impersonal—he saved himself from alienated loneliness on the one hand, and immersion in a mass life on the other. The fundamental courage of this act of the imagination may explain why in his book which is such an embrace, perhaps the fondest embrace between writer and reader in world literature, there are so many stern farewells and admonitions. Get going, he is saying, get to your own work, your own life.

My guru is running me out of the ashram. He is a father who—lucky children—really wants us to grow up, grow away, admit we aren't innocent. He lets us go. More—he requires us to bid the old camerado farewell:

> For it is not for what I have put into it that I have written this
>   book,
> Nor is it by reading it you will acquire it,

*Nor do those know me best who admire me and vauntingly praise
   me,*
*Nor will the candidates for my love (unless at the most a very few)
   prove victorious,*
*Nor will my poems do good only, they will do just as much evil,
   perhaps more,*
*For all is useless without that which you may guess at many times
   and not hit, that which I hinted at;*
Therefore release me and depart on your way.

What She
Couldn't Tell

*E*verything about Mrs. Beranek—the elaborate subterfuge of her hospitality, the dark bunker of her watchful brown
eyes—should have told me she harbored a secret. But I was incapable of recognizing a secret of her kind. I was almost thirty
when I met her, and I had piled up a number of romantic
injuries which preoccupied me. They were my only experience
of drama and dislocation. These, I thought, were secrets: shameful romantic stories that could be told—but weren't.

Real secrets hang upside-down in their bat caves, invisible in
the dark, emitting a faint radar of dread. Mrs. Beranek's secret was
like that—a signal rather than a story. She was old and foreign, she
had a serious little black mustache which made her look prim
rather than masculine. And in time I sensed with disquiet that she
needed me. These were signals enough to absorb or deflect.

In any case, it was I who came to her with a secret, or at least under a false, though benign, pretense. Mr. Henle, a member of the Seniors Poetry Group I taught at the Jewish Community Center in Saint Paul, one of the many publicly funded jobs I held in the plummy seventies, heard that I was looking for a Czech tutor. I wanted to learn the language of my grandparents, I said. *Mrs. Beranek*, he cried, *this is the person!* Later it turned out he didn't know if Mrs. Beranek was prepared to teach a language. His objective, as ever, was to do good. At ninety, still a shedder of light.

Mrs. Beranek's husband had died earlier in the year, and Mr. Henle wanted "someone sympathetic," as he said, to visit his old friend on a regular basis. Someone young, he said, pausing to assess me for a moment and apparently deciding I still qualified. No one believed I was thirty. Like everyone around me, I had attenuated the light of adolescence to the furthest, faintest point before I disappeared, past forty, into the tunnel of adulthood. No marriage, no children, no mortgage, no credit card debt, no car, no real job. I wrote poetry in the mornings, sitting on my only chair, an aluminum lawn chaise strung with thin plastic strips which left deep impressions on the back of my clothes; when I got up, it looked as if I had been whipped about the back and legs with a rod. My studio apartment had a crumbling wall which I called my Italian villa.

It was the life of the imagination. The leavings of the still buoyant Great Society supported me: I meandered among part-time jobs in community centers and nursing homes, teaching poetry, taping oral histories, gazing into the milky eyes of the elderly who were touchingly glad of the company. We had a lot in common; I was living like a pensioner myself.

As far as Mr. Henle knew, Mrs. Beranek had no one else in the world, certainly not in America. She had a heart condition, and recently had been outfitted with a pacemaker. Maybe it was the pacemaker, not the dead husband, which made her a special ward of his concern. Anyway, she should be visited, and the driver's license people had made Mr. Henle give up his car, which badly cramped his style.

"You go," he said with the decisiveness that characterized his habit of tending his dwindling band of fellow émigrés. It was 1976. Most of those left in his circle were women, widows or, like the remaining one of his three sisters with whom he had always lived, spinsters. These people had landed in Saint Paul sometime before or after the Second World War, heaved up on the Midwest's flat bosom by one version or another of the European nightmare.

Now, they were growing old, very old, in a country most of them had lived in longer than the Germany or Austria, the Poland or Czechoslovakia of their birth. In Europe they would never have met, would have seen themselves as distinct, even inimical—Jews and Gentiles, Poles, Germans, Czechs. But in Saint Paul they had been thrown together in an unlikely midwestern *Mitteleuropa*. They recognized each other, were magnetized by each other. They were from—or simply *were*—the Old World, the singular place that claimed them and exiled them all at once, but from which, even here in the American heartland, they could never truly emigrate. They were elaborately courteous to each other, and met not for cards and bunco like the working class immigrants I knew from my grandmother's circle, but to listen to the Saturday Texaco opera broadcasts. They cooked heavy, sedative meals and baked extravagant coffee cakes, they served sweet wine in thimble glasses, and toasted graciously, encouraging each other to have some more, go ahead, enjoy yourself.

Mr. Henle made all the arrangements for our first meeting.

"She is a good cook," he said reverently. I should expect cake. The hour specified—one in the afternoon—might even indicate something more substantial. He felt it impolite to inquire, but thought I might prepare myself for lunch. The event was understood to be an introductory affair; the notebook apparently was a prop but a necessary one, meant to affirm my seriousness about the language of my ancestors or maybe to belie any possible suspicion that I was Mr. Henle's minion sent on a condolence call. For that was his secret: kindness.

Mrs. Beranek lived in a high rise on the frontage road of I-94. The building, rising whitely up at the side of the freeway connecting Saint Paul and Minneapolis, was not so different from the socialist-realist *panalaky* that were forming the grim suburban wall outside Prague at the same time. Mrs. Beranek's building was a little better made, and it was a solo monolith, not one in a yawning expanse of such structures. But as I entered it the first time, I registered the place as brutal. The tenants were not being housed, but detained.

The great pale building stands there still, but in 1976 it was more exotic in its flattened affect than it appears today. Now it is oddly unremarkable. But in 1976 the great sprawl of suburban high rises, the word *condo*, the sheer height and forbidding Cold War architecture of Mrs. Beranek's building were all new to us. These high-rise warehouses, so unlike the red brick fourplexes where maiden aunts had been living amidst the scent of stewed cabbage and lavender sachet since the thirties, gave off a sinister anonymity in Saint Paul's intensely related neighborhoods. Another such looming building was being built downtown, overlooking the river. It was intended for the well-to-do. From the outside it looked a lot like Mrs. Beranek's subsidized high rise. It seemed strange not to be able to tell a poor person's house from a rich person's.

But here, on the side of the new freeway that only a few years before had scooped out the generations-old black neighborhood of Rondo and tossed it away to create the deep shoot of the super highway, Arabella Beranek, formerly of fashionable Prague Six, now made her home with African Americans displaced by the freeway and with Southeast Asians just arriving from the latest war, with welfare mothers and handicapped people on SSI.

A woman in a beige dress who always introduced herself as a nun—"I'm Sister Eileen"—had an office on the first floor, and explained that she was liaison for the residents, though it was never clear with whom or what she made liaison. She lived in the building, rent free. She had fastened on Mrs. Beranek as an island of educated refinement in her boom-box and graffiti mission. "She knows five languages, don't you?" she said to Mrs. Beranek, addressing the tenant of Unit 1803 with the peculiar awe mixed with envy that is accorded millionaires.

Our first lesson went well. There was strudel, a buttery wave rolled onto the brown sugar beach of a dough so thin it was impossible to imagine how Mrs. Beranek had cajoled it to hold its oceanic bounty of apple and raisin and cinnamon. Next to the slice of strudel on the porcelain plate, she shook from a serving spoon a heavy cumulous pile of *slehačkou*. It was the first word she taught me: whipped cream.

I was returned to the entrancing despotism of my girlhood when my dead grandmother's powers with yeast dough had ruled. We were an eating family, vassals to her lordly ways with chicken and pork roast, her flick-of-the-wrist noodles and break-your-heart piecrusts. I knew great pastry when I saw it. In Mrs. Beranek's high rise I was not simply at home, I was in the cold clutches again of an artist. She had my grandmother's same satisfied silence as she watched me eat. Eating in fact proved to be my main accomplishment as her student.

When I arrived at the high rise for my weekly lesson, it was necessary first to dial the security phone (another exotic device for us in 1976) in the corner of the vestibule. Then Mrs. Beranek, eighteen floors above in her one-bedroom, would enter a code on her wall phone which caused the big metal-and-glass door near me to emit a high, strangled sound of the kind that causes dogs to cringe. The door would then allow itself to be opened. The problem was that if I stayed on the security phone, as Mrs. Beranek instructed, by the time I made the hop to the door, the rasp had abruptly stopped, and the door perversely refused to open.

Meanwhile, other people were letting themselves in and out, making their way to the bank of elevators I could see beyond. But it was understood—signs with severe admonitions were posted on the wall—that no one without a key or an escort was allowed into the building. Beautiful young black girls flounced past with their keys, dismissing me with neutral disdain as they slammed the door in my face. Sister Eileen, trolling the corridors, often came to my rescue. "I think it's wonderful you're studying your grandparents' language," she said approvingly. "Looking for your roots."

When I stepped out of the elevator on the eighteenth floor, Mrs. Beranek was always waiting for me. She even had my grandmother's body, small, round, the stout build of a generalissimo, and she conducted me back to her apartment as if there were no time to spare before maneuvers began. I was directed to the table in the dining area, a corner of the living room near the kitchen. There was a view of the Montgomery Ward parking lot and a car dealership beyond.

The tabletop, made of Formica, was covered with a lace cloth. A low cut-glass bowl held a bundle of plastic ivy leaves. The sugar bowl was large, and the table was always set. A solitary cup and saucer sat at Mrs. Beranek's place at the head of the table. My place, facing the sideboard below the window, held the works—dinner plate, soup bowl, salad plate, cup, saucer, glass, silver. "First," she always said, "we eat." Then she disappeared into the kitchen.

She had herded a collection of framed photographs onto the sideboard. Most of them were recent—pictures she had identified for me as Bonnie, her husband's last nurse and Bonnie's large family, snapshots of her husband looking thin and, I thought, weak. He had died, Mrs Beranek told me, of congestive heart failure and emphysema. She could see him fading right before her eyes. "But we were happy," she said proudly, "right to the end. Very happy." She picked up a picture frame, and dusted the glass with the corner of her apron, unconsciously stroking his face. The face in the photograph looked severe, even sour. But maybe, I thought, that was the illness. There were a few older pictures, including a wedding portrait from the twenties. The satin train of Mrs. Beranek's dress, carrying forward the *slehačkou* motif, was swirled in a creamy puddle at the feet of the smug-looking bridal couple.

A large black-and-white photograph dominated the group, propped in a possibly real silver frame. It was clearly from a later period, the women wearing the short-skirted, square-shouldered suits of the forties. This small group, apparently on vacation but dressed to the nines, stood on a terrace before a hotel, mountains (the Tatras, I learned later) spiking grandly behind them.

I would give a lot to have that picture before me now. For one thing, though I can clearly see Mr. Beranek standing straight, his black hair slicked back, I cannot remember if he was wearing his uniform as an officer in the Czechoslovak Army or was dressed in a civilian suit. This would be a valuable distinction. The Sam Brown leather belt running diagonally across his chest one day is perversely supplanted the next time I bring the picture to mind by a smoky three-piece suit with a high-buttoned waist-coat. I can see the dull brass on the leather belt—but also the black poker-chip buttons that punctuate the tweedy waistcoat. Tricks of memory. But the dark hat Mrs. Beranek wore—that snaps back in disturbing focus, real, not remembered. It is cocked sharply over her left brow, casting a bold eye in shadow.

When was it, I now wonder, that I became suspicious of the hat? It was an unsettling hat. I regarded with vague disquiet its aggressive angle shadowing Mrs. Beranek's smiling face. But I didn't pursue the thought. I kept spooning in the *slehačkou,* licking buttery crumbs off my fingers while I copied irregular verbs into my notebook week after week.

Mr. Henle's plan was working. I was spending a lot of time with Mrs. Beranek. I borrowed my mother's car and drove her to the Henles' for lunch, I took her to the bank, I delivered her to the German cultural club for the fall sauerkraut dinner, she came home with me for Thanksgiving. I took her to Mass now and again. I got in the habit of taking her grocery shopping. She was a wily shopper, her purse bulging with carefully scissored news-paper coupons which she paid out at the checkout counter like a stack of chips at a casino. She was gleeful about her strategic buy-ing, by turns petulant over the price of peaches and contemptu-ous of what the supermarket thought she would pay for a cut-up chicken. Ha! She'd cut up her own chicken. I drove her all over town, stalking deals, running up mileage on my mother's car.

In the spring we went to the cemetery where her husband was buried. It was the Catholic cemetery; my grandmother and grandfather were buried there too, under a pine tree in an old, shady section I had always found pleasant. Mrs. Beranek had purchased an imposing marker for her husband in the bright tree-less area full of recent monuments where in summer patches of the grass burned brown. She had engraved on the monument not only Mr. Beranek's name and dates but her own name and birth date, followed by an eloquent hyphen waiting in the stone like a held breath.

She always wept a bit at the cemetery. Once she clutched my arm as we approached the big gray granite stone, and asked desperately, "It isn't possible—it isn't, is it?—that after everything, we will not meet again? We must meet again. Don't you think we must?" The mustache quivered fiercely.

"Of course," I answered immediately. She looked at me with misgiving.

"We must meet again," she replied furiously, as if I had contradicted her. She stood in the unforgiving sun, not a tree to shade the place, frantic with disbelief at his disappearance. She was waiting impatiently in the echoing terminal of her grief until, as she knew he soon must, he came to retrieve her.

She doled out her story a little at a time. She had been an opera singer. This, and her position in Prague's *haute bourgeoisie* explained all the languages. She worked for the Americans in Germany after the war, translating from German and Czech, though her French and Italian were just as good. She said it was the best job she ever had. When she and her husband landed finally in Saint Paul, middle-aged and penniless in the early

1950s, they both found jobs at the Toni factory, home of the famous (to us) Tonette home permanent. At first she worked on the line; eventually she moved to an office job. It was never clear to me what her husband did there, or why they ended up in Saint Paul, having entered the country in New Orleans. They hung on to their Tonette jobs for dear life; she spoke of the Toni Company patriotically, as if by working for the cosmetics industry she and her husband had done national service, serving their adopted country in its time of need.

Apparently she had not worked in Prague. She was not even quite a professional singer, it seems, though she had trained for the opera. Saint-Saëns, she said, wanted her to be the first Mélisande in *Pelléas et Mélisande*. Saint-Saëns! I was all agog. She offered no more. She had turned down Saint-Saëns in order to marry Mr. Beranek. I was given to understand that theirs had been a great love, that between Saint-Saëns and Mr. Beranek there had been no contest.

And how did she spend her days after her marriage, during the fifteen years of the First Republic before Hitler invaded Czechoslovakia? She paused, shaking her head in mild wonder at this other life which was improbable now even to her. "I don't know," she said. After a moment, "I believe I planned what we would have for dinner."

An absurd life, lazy and ordered and harmless. There was a small staff—a cook and a maid. The flat was large, weighted with Biedermeier. She practiced her singing. She read novels. She met her friends for coffee in the afternoon. In the evening there was the theater or an opera. Prague then was like Montreal, a dual-culture city, and they went to plays at the German and the Czech theaters. It was a dreamy existence, playing house, gossiping, warbling a bit in the music room, keeping up her languages. No children. "It was not possible for us," she said, opening and shut-

ting the subject. "People without children have the closest mar-
riages," she added. "I was never lonely."

Until now, of course. Sometimes she brought out her picture
albums and we looked over them together. Her husband, again
with the smug, turning-sour face, in his Army uniform, in a
buffed studio photograph from the early thirties; pages of snapshots from Toni Company annual picnics, others from German
cultural club gatherings. She was Czech, not German, but in
Saint Paul it seemed not to matter. She liked to use her German.
It was the language she and Mr. Henle and his sister used when
I wasn't around. Though she was Catholic, she sometimes went
with them to Jewish Community Center events.

One day she shyly, proudly presented a yellowed feature
piece, dating from the early 1950s, from the *St. Paul Pioneer Press*
which was pasted into an album. Mrs. Beranek (dark-haired,
robust, not yet an old lady) beamed from a desk at the Toni
Company. A thin but not yet gaunt Mr. Beranek stood behind
her, looking mildly, if a bit uncomfortably, into the camera. The
article was bannered with a rich anti-Communist scream of a
headline which I no longer remember. The Beraneks told of
escaping from the Reds—they could not live in such a prison as
their country had become, the article said, and had risked everything to get to freedom. That is, to Minnesota, to us.

Mrs. Beranek's languages were noted as if they comprised a
fabulous foreign bank account she had somehow managed to
sneak across the border when she had fled in the night, dogs
snapping at her heels. The courage and resourcefulness of their
passion for freedom, the reporter wrote, had brought them at last
to our midst. They acknowledged the terrible life behind the
Iron Curtain, and their vast relief in arriving in a free land, their
hope of making new lives in service to the Toni Company. They
wanted people to know how thankful they were. They hoped to

be useful, productive citizens in their new country, they said, ending the piece on an oddly socialist sentiment.

In another album Mrs. Beranek had mounted a large, more recent picture that looked like the publicity glossy of an actress. Which is exactly what it was. "My cousin's daughter," she said. "She's an actress in Prague. When she can get work." The face was Liv Ullman lovely, lyrical and strong. "You can meet her when you go back to Prague."

I had been to Prague the year before, and I was crazy to return. This was the point of studying Czech. I said—and believed—that my passion for the city had to do with my grandparents, my *roots*, as Sister Eileen said so approvingly. But it was the city's grainy noir-ish quality which had captivated me. It was the opposite of family feeling that propelled me there. I was after a dark otherness.

Prague entered me the way bad weather invades a landscape, haunting and enshrining a place more powerfully than a sunny day ever can. I was after that bad weather, the endless drizzle of history, though I didn't understand that I had touched the broken heart of the century in the city's crumbling baroque buildings and grimy coal-dust air. I told Mrs. Beranek that Prague was beautiful. Wasn't that why people went to Europe? For the beauty? Except in the seventies nobody much went to Prague. It was the first European city I saw, and I experienced it in its isolation and humiliation. I traveled like a sleepwalker, drawn out of sun-and-snow Minnesota, going alone, I knew not why, into the night strangeness of the gray-and-smudged-gold Bohemian capital. After Prague, I took a train to Paris, and was secretly ashamed that the city of lights meant nothing, nothing. I couldn't see it. I stood before the Arc de Triomphe, and said in my bored heart, *So?* Give me back the ruined gold of Praha.

It is easier now, after the Cold War, to understand what I

sought there, what secrets and fascinations that part of the world held in its closed fist for "the West." The land of Mozart and the concentration camps, beer and bootjacks. All that was "behind the Iron Curtain," as we said for decades, relying on that most eloquent of political metaphors to hide it all and say it all. The east wing of the great European mansion was closed off, we really thought, forever, the furniture shrouded in dusty muslin, all the relatives lost or scattered. For Mrs. Beranek it was forever. "Oh no," she said, horrified, "I would never go back." The freedom-lover who had fled with only a rucksack on her back, shuddered at the thought.

Mr. Henle, I reminded her, had gone back. The Lutheran minister of Ulm, his hometown, had invited him and his remaining sister back to Germany. At first Mr. Henle had refused. How could he go back? But after a while he decided, yes, it was time. "There must be forgiveness," he told me.

He said this not as a sentiment or an earnest wish, but as a fact, pronouncing it like the bottom-line accountant he had been in his American cousin's furniture store since he arrived from Europe. The strict economy of history required pardon— not because there was no guilt to be assigned or no abiding outrage in the human heart, but because the force of time pushed green shoots out of the bloodied earth, and Mr. Henle bowed his gaunt head respectfully to the new growth. The future, uncaring though it was, had its rights. This was his attitude, profoundly unsentimental yet not cynical. He refused rage, it seemed, because it turned too surely into piety. He did not like the word *Holocaust*. He did not approve of the package, the tidiness the word made of chaos, bundling up so much in its furious sound. Yet clearly, he remembered everything that was lost to him. He had the lined, ascetic face of a scholar who pondered alone.

He and his sister had returned to Ulm the previous year. They were feted like heroes—or perhaps like the dead risen again to life. So many had not come back, but here they were, the Henles, owners once upon a time of the city's best dry goods store—back, alive. Well, two of them, anyway. He told the story of the trip without delight or triumph, without bitterness. He did not dwell on psychological "closure" or any such fluff. It seemed that he had gone, finally, from that most neutral but also most galvanizing of human instincts: he was curious.

"Well, the Henles are Jewish," Mrs. Beranek said. "They can go back." The soured look, the one in her husband's formal portraits from before the war, touched her face, making the little black mustache seem, for once, sinister. "Everyone feels sorry for the Jews."

Like the photograph of the Tatra mountains where the unsettling dark hat angled aggressively over her bold eye—yes, I realized, it was a bold eye, even saucy!—this remark grazed me. *Everyone feels sorry for the Jews.* I thrust the remark away, fended it off like an unwanted intimacy. It sent the same signal the hat sent. It winked its terrible wink. It beckoned.

If only we had fought, we could have beat the Germans. This was her Czech Army officer husband's belief, a faith she repeated as fact. If, in 1938, the Czechs had gone to war against the German annexation of their border territory, instead of collapsing into occupation, they would have beat the Germans.

Without the help of England and France? (I couldn't help asking).

Without their help. The black mustache pursed decisively. The generalissimo of the kitchen spoke from the high command of her Army officer husband, her five European languages flying their flags. Americans did not understand these things.

That took care of the Second World War. There was no more to it. No newspaper clippings in the album, no stories she felt compelled to tell. The war, to her, was the held breath of the Czech nation, as if the whole occupation had been a blank, an insult without incident.

Then the war was over. Oh, that was the worst, *after* the war. The images pulsed across the lace-covered table, where I sat behind my notebook and my hazelnut torte. People—neighbors!—jumped on the faces of Germans thrown into the streets. Jumped with boots! A head soaking in rain and blood and gasoline just lying there in the gutter outside her apartment building. No body, just the smashed face. People spitting. Ordinary people went into German homes; they killed them in their beds, threw them out their windows. Stole things. As if they were dogs, oh much worse than the way a dog is treated.

Yes, she agreed, people were angry after the Nazi occupation. "But these were human beings too," she said. She fastened me with a pleading look so strange I remember it more absolutely than her voice. *These were human beings too.*

I nodded, I clucked along, I agreed, my mouth full of hazelnut ganache, that the Germans too were human beings. The smashed head in the street, ground down by a Czech boot was reason enough to shudder.

But I knew then, years before I allowed myself to turn back to that scene in memory—not the memory of her bloodied Prague street, but the scene of the two of us, meeting in the sugar-haze of our lesson over her lace-covered Formica table—that this postwar horror was not what her eyes were pleading with me to understand. How strange is the communication of a secret when it cannot speak, when the eyes must send their inchoate signal, asking for—what?

For forgiveness. Absolution. But maybe these words are too crudely decorous for what she sought. She wanted out. She was locked up with something, in something. An oil-and-water mixture of shame and fury swam in her eyes, seeking an understanding she could not hope to find. She did not deserve this! her locked-on-me eyes were saying. She had never looked at me like this, nobody ever has. I felt searched. She wished me to acquiesce to some statement she could not utter, to read her invisible ink. Was it a confession she had in mind? She was trying to pry something out of a reticence so profound it had become a pledge. A pledge to whom?

"During the War, my husband . . . " she said, looking down for an instant. I knew instinctively that she was going to tell me something she had never told anyone, that we were poised together over an abyss where she had stood before only with her husband until this earnest Czech language student came to sit at her table, filling up on refined sugar, a nice American girl with no ax to grind, who had seen nothing but the gloomy Iron Curtain surface of her city and called it beauty. Tell *her*.

A canny foreknowledge flooded me. I snapped alert as a pointer in a cornfield of pheasant. This was what all the trips to the grocery store had been for, the chauffeuring and the cemetery visits, even the weekly Czech lessons and my gushing flattery about her baking, though I hadn't realized it. I was not kind as Mr. Henle was kind, simply and as a matter of character. I had been waiting for this from the first lesson, the spill-the-beans moment that had been winking at me under the shadow of her dark wartime hat from the first day. "Yes?" I said gently prodding, beckoning her to risk it, to trust me over here across the table in earnest, naive America. *Yes, Mrs. Beranek?* . . .

And in speaking broke the spell forever.

She told me nothing. "No, I cannot, never mind," she said, pulling away. The best she could give me was to acknowledge that she *was* holding something back, that I was right in presuming she had almost, almost . . .

She removed her heavy glasses and covered her eyes for a long moment. There may have been tears, but I think it was a drier, more hopeless moment. She kept her crumpled face in her hands. I held my breath behind the hazelnut torte, trying desperately to figure out how to coax her back to the edge of utterance where we had been standing together only a moment before, where she might still tumble, allowing her terrible truth to fall into my waiting arms.

On a raw March night almost a year later, Sister Eileen called around ten o'clock. She had a key to the apartment, she said, but she was afraid to go in by herself. She wanted me to come quickly.

For once when I arrived at the high rise I didn't need to be buzzed in. Sister Eileen was waiting at the big glass and metal door. We went up together in the elevator. "I have a key," she said again. "I have a master key to all the apartments. Most people aren't aware of that." She seemed more nervous than a nun should be, I thought, in the face of . . .

We could hear the television when we got to Mrs. Beranek's door. This could be a good sign—or a bad sign. Sister Eileen knocked, timidly. Nothing. I stepped forward and beat loudly on the hollow-core door. "You better open it," I said finally. It seemed I was in charge, that Sister Eileen wanted me to take command.

And there she was, slumped heavily before the television on the lumpy tweed couch in the little living room, the sports news blasting. Her eyes were closed, thank God. Her legs were splayed slightly apart like an exhausted Siegel figure waiting at a bus stop after the night shift, the head bent down. But not, we both knew instantly, sleeping.

I turned the television off. Then wished I hadn't. The noise had a reassuring buoyancy to it, a satisfying surface. Sister Eileen made for the door. She was going to call an ambulance from her own apartment. "You wait here," she said, suddenly taking away the command I thought she had given me.

I almost turned the television back on. I wasn't afraid, being alone with her—not Mrs. Beranek anymore, suddenly "the body"—but the silence felt indecent. It was all too casual, as if death were a brief item tacked on at the end of a broadcast on a slow news day. It seemed wrong to look at her, and I couldn't bring myself to touch her. I found a clean pastel sheet in the bedroom dresser and draped it over her from head to foot, and then felt foolish—what was wrong with letting her just be there, sitting? But once I had covered her, I couldn't bring myself to undrape her. It wasn't even a real gesture, just something I got from the movies—pulling the sheet up over the face of the dead heroine.

As I shook out the sheet to cover her, an absurd response, my only authentic one, floated over my mind: *What happened to all the languages?* As if she had not died, but had been robbed. As if someone should be apprehended and held accountable for this theft. I couldn't get the thought out of my mind—that the languages had been abducted. It was her Czech and German I mourned for, her operatic Italian and the French she had chosen not to sing for Saint-Saëns. The wealth she had managed to smuggle out of her destroyed Europe, stored here where no one would think of looking, in the high rise on the side of a midwestern freeway, marooned in English with Sister Eileen and me.

I looked at the sheeted figure with a kind of awe, but I was not sad and I was sorry about that. I had not liked her, I realized, and I knew it was too bad that it was me she got at the end, not a good person like nurse Bonnie who had seen her husband to his end, but me who stood above her with my cold heart and my suspicions, covering her up like a shameful thing, waiting for someone to take her away.

I went back to Prague later that year. I could now read the difference between the words on the men's room and the women's toilets. This, roughly, was the extent of my Czech after my months of lessons. It was 1977, still the deep dark days in Prague.

I looked up the actress cousin whose movie-star glossy I had seen in Mrs. Beranek's album. We met outside in Old Town Square, below the black Art Nouveau monument of Jan Hus, the great Czech martyr for the truth, erected during the early optimistic years of the First Republic. The sun was shining, I remember, and the actress (her name refuses to come back) was a little older than I had expected and not glamorous. She lived with her parents, in an apartment she also shared with her ex-husband and his current girlfriend. A Czech arrangement, real estate deciding everything.

She told me she had been in a movie with Albert Finney, a speaking part in an Anglo-Czech co-production in the hopeful time before 1968. Now she rarely got calls, except for a little radio work. She stayed at home and read novels. She was pale, still beautiful, but drab somehow, as if she no longer counted herself in. She had only known Mrs. Beranek and her husband when she was very small. She hardly had a real memory of either of them.

I asked when they had left the country.

After the war, she said. She hesitated a moment.

"You mean 1948?" I asked. It was the year of the Communist coup in Prague.

She looked at me and decided. "1945," she said.

Dates are eloquent. We both knew that leaving in 1945 was incriminating. A good Czech stayed after the liberation in '45—and a good Czech might leave in '48, the year of the Communist coup. But a good Czech, a blameless Czech, did not run for her life in 1945, after the liberation.

I told her I had suspected something. Yes, she said. But she too was in the dark, did not know exactly what it was—I sensed she really did not know. But she used the word: *collaborator*. Mr. Beranek had done—what? Something, something. He had been arrested right after the war. Somehow they had bribed their way out in the very early days, and had indeed fled in secret over the border into Germany, dogs at their heels. As Mrs. Beranek said, she had worked for the Americans until they managed to get to America. But they were not anti-Communists, had not fled from the Reds. The story in the *Pioneer Press* from the fifties, the two of them at their Toni Company jobs, dealing out their escape story to St. Paul readers shivering a delicious Cold War shiver—it was all a fiction, a great woolly tale they pulled up over their own heads as well as ours.

Mrs. Beranek, I told the actress, had started to tell me something once. But had stopped, had thought better of trusting me.

I described the vacation picture in the Tatras, the mid-war good times, the too-fashionable hat. She was having the time of her life, I said.

The actress nodded. "They were in some kind of trouble," she said. It was something Mr. Beranek had done during the war. It was a long time ago and nobody wanted to talk about it.

Then she asked me about American movies, and the conversation took another turn, away from the war and whatever secret I would never know, and into the unlived life that was her own secret, her lovely eyes wistful and wry, knowing she would never play opposite Albert Finney again. "He used to call me cupcake," she said. "We joked around." She paused. We were both leaning against the base of the Jan Hus statue. "It was a dream once," she said finally. "But it wasn't meant to be."

Sister Eileen told me not to expect any money. Money! Why would I expect any money? Sister Eileen eyed me closely. "Bonnie gets all the money," she said. "Nobody else gets anything." It was clear she was hurt.

I thought of fabulous sums, the Toni Company heiress living in subsidized housing, her bank accounts swelling in secret, all of it left to a kind nurse. A morality tale: Be nice, it pays. It turned out there was $20,000, and it all did go to Bonnie.

But Sister Eileen was wrong. There was something for me. Bonnie called me after I got back from Prague, and said Mrs. Beranek had wanted me to have her Prague album, the photographs of Pliček, somber cityscapes of empty streets and drear river embankments, a city of sleepers, not dreamers, a landscape of absence, rather than remembrance. A big headachy book of strangely mute photographs, withholding even as they presented the images of the beloved city, the bad-weather Prague I was after.

*T*ime, we like to say, cures all. But maybe the old saying doesn't mean time heals. Time cures a secret in its brine, keeping it and finally, paradoxically, destroying it. Nothing is left in that salt solution but the pain or rage, the biting shame that lodged it there. Even they are diluted or denied.

Sufficient time must pass, we are told, after a great or defining experience in order to write history—personal or otherwise. Passions must cool. The necessary distance must be achieved. But what, really, is left to tell from the position of this exemplary coolness? Occasionally an undissolved sliver floats up from the corrosive murk to pierce and poison the heart. But nothing is left of the thing itself. The secret has completed its vocation of extinction. It is gone, cured. Lost in its corrosive element.

If you write about me one day, Mrs. Beranek had said, cannily prophetic, *don't use my real name*. We were sitting together at the lace-covered Formica table, drinking sugared coffee, avoiding the Czech lesson as we often did.

She was serious. I teased her, but the little black mustache pursed and quivered. She was adamant, made me promise.

"What shall I call you then?" I asked.

Beranek, she said brightly, as if she had her pseudonym at the ready all along, just waiting. *That was my husband's idea. That's what you should call me—Mrs. Beranek*. She added coyly, *It means little lamb*.

She smiled a deep and private smile, luxuriating in her faithful silence as she gazed out the window, past Ward's and the car dealership, to a better time and the abiding radiance of her innocence.

Czeslaw Milosz and Memory

I

For good or more often for bad, we in the West tend to associate the recollection of the personal past with nostalgia. But an impulse removed from this luscious *temps perdu* sensation informs the memoirs of the Polish poet Czeslaw Milosz. He is not alone in his willfully impersonal use of personal memory. The novels of the Czech writers Milan Kundera and Josef Škvořecky (like Milosz, exiles of the Cold War era) address the impersonality of memory, as do the accounts, now forming a genre of their own, by survivors of the concentration camps of the century.

Remembrance in these writers is less strictly personal than it is in most American autobiography, though the uncanny and formative moments of a life remain, as in any memoir, the basis of the work. But for these writers the past is the nation's finally, not the family's, as it so typically is in American memoir. The brush strokes are those of history, rather than autobiograp

Seen in this light, the work of memory becomes politically dynamic, and personal testimony approaches danger, for its purpose becomes not only elegy but survival. It is the survival of something larger than the author's self or even of a beloved, departed past. At stake is the survival of memory itself. In such works, memory lives to serve history.

And how else could it be in what used to be called "the other Europe," the land of the concentration camp, the massacred villages and lost populations? But the swerve away from nostalgia antedates that genocide. It has to do, I think, with being small—a feature of existence that existed before the camps, and remained even through the Iron Curtain period and its astonishing late-century meltdown.

Memory, for a small nation (or one denied sovereignty) *is* the nation. And the first, most complete, shared memory of a nation is its language. In fact, preserving the native tongue is traditionally the basic political act of an endangered nation, a classic rallying point. At the root of utterance, language conspires to be political, cohesive of the nation, a linguistic fortress preserving those gathered within it.

Coming from such a nation—where borders are erased and redrawn within a generation, where countries cease to exist on maps or exist only on maps, where even the oppressor isn't a constant (Is Germany on the march? No? Then Poland? Russia?)—a writer has reason to feel jumpy when contemplating the notion of "identity." The solution of the contemporary American imagination in regard to identity is to "seek the self," uncovering its hidden psychology, to "get in touch with the unconscious." This must seem thin gruel to writers from the marginalized nations of Europe.

It certainly does to Milosz, who remarks in the introduction to his memoir, *Native Realm,* "I mistrust the probings into the

subconscious that are so honored in our day." This sort of statement betrays a touchiness about personal revelation that is foreign to the habits of the American imagination. From Whitman's
"Song of Myself" to the feminist motto that "the personal is
political," the American sensibility has been happy—or at least
thoroughly absorbed—in making a world of the self.

Of his own reticence, Milosz simply says: "There is nothing
degrading in our fundamental incapacity to lay bare all the particulars of our fate." His point seems to be that there is no such
thing as *telling all*. There remains, however, the necessity to tell.
This necessity, coupled with "our fundamental incapacity to lay
bare all the particulars of our fate," is in fact the mother of form:

> If it were any different, if that chaotic richness, in the pres-
> ence of which our faculties are like a circle of lantern light
> in the darkness, did not exist, we would not constantly be
> aspiring to form achieved by a process of elimination, and
> probably the art of writing would disappear.

In writing his memoir, Milosz does not work with anecdo-
tal reminiscence: he is *after* something different from a story in
the usual narrative sense. "Another method," he says, "is possible."
This other method for memoir is his alternative to the "probings" that so often leave literature in the West with a surfeit of
self and an "authenticity" that seems strangely counterfeit.
"Instead of thrusting the individual into the foreground," Milosz
says,

> one can focus attention on the background, looking upon
> oneself as a sociological phenomenon. Inner experience, as it
> is preserved in the memory, will then be evaluated in the
> perspective of the changes one's milieu has undergone. The

passing over of certain periods important for oneself, but requiring too personal an explanation, will be a token of respect for those undergrounds that exist in all of us and that are better left in peace. . . .

So, what are you trying to cover up? the American mind can't help wondering. And what's "too personal"? We read *People* magazine at the checkout counter; we can't get enough of each other's personal lives. Or what we suppose to be personal.

But it is just this absence of reticence that saps American autobiography and trivializes American memory. No doubt, it also accounts for our notorious ahistorical sensibility. The self is the story; history is just landscape. The impersonality Milosz wishes to establish as memoir's proper "method" is antithetical to American psychological autobiography, but for that reason it is refreshing, even a possible restorative for the fevered American approach.

Milosz hinges the personal story to the history of the nation. The fusion of these two narrations—the one intimate, the other public—creates a powerful call and reply which achieves poetic form. It is a *relationship*—that bruised word of our own relentlessly psychological culture, reclaimed by the "impersonal" method Milosz suggests.

The relation works not only as connection but as detachment. The distance created by his aloofness from "probing" gives the self elbow room. Milosz becomes a moving figure, an actor whose gestures are eloquent because they indicate something beyond himself. He has located the best grace of memoir: a method which allows the self to function not as a source or a subject, but as an instrument for rendering the world. In *Native Realm* Milosz does not seek a self; he seeks to use a self. In this, of course, he approaches the spiritual preserve of myth—some-

How to associate yourself as a typical/Absentee Father

thing graver and more stately than fiction, but a work of the imagination nonetheless.

Throughout his memoir Milosz refers to himself as "a typical Eastern European." Such a designation does not require him to deny either his Polish or Lithuanian heritage. This Eastern European type, he says,

My rel. or lack thereof w/ my father + mother + her could write it in "phases" of ea. child

> can be boiled down to a lack of form—both inner and outer. His good qualities—intellectual avidity, fervor in discussion, a sense of irony, freshness of feeling, spatial (or geographical) fantasy—derive from a basic weakness: he always remains an adolescent, governed by a sudden ebb or flow of inner chaos.

The type, in other words, doesn't quite exist, isn't quite *there*; its qualities include formlessness—a perfect invitation to a writer who, after all, must *make* something. And by this act of making he is inevitably committed to form. Interestingly, this Eastern European formlessness bears a striking resemblance to the classic American quest for identity. While the American pattern is to seek for itself in the absence of long history, the Eastern European is lost in a welter of (usually tragic, heroic) history. But the result is oddly similar: the absence of a clearly established national self.

rather than strict chronology or by that way the end is not revealed too early

The intimacy Milosz extends as a memoirist, while aloof ("this is not a book of feelings," he says), is keen with detail. Ideology, not to mention the awful specificity of his experience of history, has made him allergic to imprecision. Nor does a life lived near genocide have the luxury of a vague, cloudy guilt: "The greatest ally of any ideology is, of course, the feeling of guilt, which is so highly developed in modern man that it saps his belief in the value of his own perceptions and judgments."

As a poet, Milosz knows that "to see and to describe" (as he says in his 1980 Nobel Lecture) is his business. That is the work of attending to detail. His subject in *Native Realm* is history, its effects and uses, its wounds and power, but his genre remains the personal memoir. For good reason:

> . . . unless we can relate it to ourselves personally, history will always be more or less of an abstraction, and its content the clash of impersonal forces and ideas. Although generalizations are necessary to order its vast, chaotic material, they kill the individual detail that tends to stray from the schema. Doubtless every family archive that perishes, every account book that is burned, every effacement of the past reinforces classifications and ideas at the expense of reality. Afterward, all that remains of entire centuries is a kind of popular digest. And not one of us today is immune to that contagion.

This reverent attitude toward the specific family past holds the cause of accuracy as sacred. But such solemnizing of the family experience is employed not for the location of a self—not only personal letters, but account books are sacred in Milosz's list of vulnerable reality. This reverence for detail and the fragments of personal experience is necessary for one who is determined to be useful by being representative:

> The awareness of one's origins is like an anchor line plunged into the deep, keeping one within a certain range. Without it, historical intuition is virtually impossible.

His family, which he traces in *Native Realm* from 1580, was gentry. By the time Milosz was born (1911), this caste designation apparently meant not wealth or unusual prestige, but an association with a historical identity. He describes this national identity as a "melange of Polish, Lithuanian, and German blood," which included the likelihood of becoming an intellectual: In Poland "the intelligentsia . . . was sociologically linked to the gentry." In other words, his family heritage *is* to be "historical," to be profoundly aware of the small nations of Eastern Europe. The family business is history. He describes his sense of dislocation from this rich history, when in postwar settings in the West he was percieved as a product of a Communist country, a minion of the proletarian mass:

> At many a reception in Washington or in Paris, where enthusiastic ladies would approach a Red with a delicious shiver, I felt that I was only half-present. Too many shadows enveloped me: the clanking of sabers, the rustling of Renaissance gowns, the fragrance of old houses full of animal hides, hunting arms, coaches, rusted armor; and this robbed what was going on around me of some of its reality.

A further effect of this consciousness of his background is the distance it gives him. It is a distance akin to poetic objectivity, and in addition to affecting the living of his life, it also influ- ences his *observing* the life: "One should appreciate, after all, the advantages of one's origin. Its worth lies in the power it gives one to detach oneself from the present moment." This apparently casual assumption is at exact odds with a standard American assumption about autobiography: that the personal or family past, plumbed and reabsorbed as conscious narrative (whether written in a book or told in a therapist's office, spinning the tale aloud to the air), clarifies, even reveals "the present moment."

The American assumption is almost always psychological, and therefore personal. There is a throb toward (personal) salvation beating within American autobiography. Milosz's assumption is superficially cooler, harder. Put another way, it is more elemental. For him, the awareness of a rich and complex "origin" necessarily dilutes some of the paralyzing power of the present: something else is always tugging at consciousness, something neither wholly familial nor wholly abstract. This presence which lies at the heart of the experience of memory is *both* personal and impersonal. This double nature of his memory, which Milosz says caused his post-War experience in the West to be "robbed" of some of its "reality," is, from an American middle-class perspective, an enriching and intensifying of reality. For Americans, except for those who write memoir out of specific historical experience (Philip Caputo writing about the Vietnam War, for example), the family and personal psychology dominate "reality." And of course limit it, constrain it, and finally, inflate it.

When Milosz gives a personal detail, he leaves it to find its way in the rich environment of history. His "personal reminiscences" do not charm—and not simply because they are often part of a tragic context. He just doesn't manipulate detail as most memoirists do; his details must raise their own voices to be eloquent—he does not impose his will upon them. Here he is ending a chapter:

I had already left my city (Vilno) when the Germans murdered its Jews. For that purpose they chose Ponary, a forest of oaks in the hills, the place where we went on school and university excursions. . . . An organization of Jewish fighters in the ghetto resisted. I knew a man who had never imagined he would be one of the leaders in that battle, but who fought only so that he might die without begging for mercy. He was a lawyer with an athletic build who liked to recite Mayakovsky's poems while drinking vodka. Although he was not a Communist, he adored this poet of revolution and knew perhaps half of his works by heart. To this day, I can see his hairy wrist with the gold watchband gesturing in measured movements to the rhythm of the lines.

That glinting wrist, gesturing to accent a line of poetry, carries the weight of a city's destroyed population.

Or here, from a happier time:

When I reached adolescence, I carried inside me a museum of mobile and grimacing images: blood-smeared Seryozha, a sailor with a dagger, commissars in leather jackets, Lena, a German sergeant directing an orchestra, Lithuanian riflemen from paramilitary units, and these were mingled with a throng of peasants—smugglers and hunters, Mary Pickford, Alaskan fur trappers, and my drawing instructor.

Some of these figures remain obscure (who is the drawing instructor?), but that's the point: they are idiosyncratic images, meant to float. Their very mystery is proof of their authenticity. They are *in there,* part of the packed past which is neither something to explain away nor manipulate into a too-fine feeling: Milosz won't be nostalgic, just as he won't be ideological. He is a writer of the middle territory caught between the *temps perdu* of the West and the political theories of the ideological East, clutching the shards of his historical experience as a touchstone of reality.

Still, his unwillingness to be defined by politics does not mean that he will "forgo a discussion of ideological quarrels. That would be a very meager portrait of a concrete time and place." Once again, he invokes an impersonal reason: It is the time and place, not his own identity, which require his involvement in ideology. This acquiescence to one's arbitrary *placement* (in "a concrete time and place") may be the greatest, and to an American, most *foreign*, aspect of Milosz's memoir. Perhaps the only great autobiographies are those which display this acquiescence to the arbitrary facts of birth and circumstances. *The Autobiography of Malcolm X* is such a book. Like *Native Realm* (though without invoking any theory of memoir as Milosz does), Malcolm's voice in the *Autobiography* is bred of history, not of the individual.

Just as he promises, Milosz's memoir is that of an Eastern European ("I consider myself a typical Eastern European"); of a Catholic ("One never stops being a member of the Catholic Church. This is what her doctrine teaches and what the two attitudes of acceptance and opposition confirm"); of a poet ("My nature demanded that I bend my knee before something or someone—to praise"); of a leftist who did not have the luxury of indecision ("Happy are they who can avoid radical choices"); of a provincial (who felt himself and other provincial Eastern Europeans to be "burdened with a longing for a homeland other than the one assigned to them from birth"); of a catastrophist (in his poems "there was terror . . . and a foreboding of what was to come").

In addition to all these selves, there is the constantly renewed naive or student self, always seeking (and finding) a mentor: teachers in school, of course; his relative, the French language poet Oscar Milosz (certainly the most important figure of his poetic development); a postwar Polish intellectual he calls Tiger, who exemplifies the conflicts of that period in Poland; and—surprise—Einstein in a fascinating cameo appearance as Milosz contemplates his "defection" to the United States.

Many selves in a vast history. And true to his sense of his

"method" for autobiography, these representative selves do attain *form*, they coalesce. The figure they become—indeed must become in order to serve the purpose of protagonist for history—is the pilgrim. The old hero of fairy tale, refashioned.

II

For many centuries, while kingdoms rose and fell along the shores of the Mediterranean and countless generations handed down their refined pleasures and vices, my native land was a virgin forest whose only visitors were the few Viking ships that landed on the coast. Situated beyond the compass of maps, it was more legendary than real.

So *Native Realm* begins—very like a fairy tale. Milosz could hardly have come up with a beginning closer to "Once upon a time . . ." The focus is on the land, not the author's birth: Geography is the first self.

He is speaking here of Lithuania which, given its history, *is* rather like speaking of a mythic, unreal kingdom. We learn in *Native Realm* that Lithuania has often "not existed," and that its landlords have been various. Milosz himself has an appropriately shadowy connection to his first homeland:

My family [he says in his Nobel Lecture] in the sixteenth century already spoke Polish, just as many families in Finland spoke Swedish and in Ireland English; so I am a Polish, not a Lithuanian, poet.

To be and yet not to be a native son, to be and yet not to be a nation—these are fascinating ambiguities that positively require the fashioning hand of the imagination to make something of them. They draw the mind past the immediate memories of family, beyond even a historical instinct, to a primary identity which, while not exactly racial, feels almost as basic.

In a way—the best way—Milosz is a regionalist. It is an allegiance to what he calls, in his Nobel Lecture, "that disorderly, illogical humanity, [which is] so often branded as ridiculous because of its parochial attachments and loyalties." In writing about his neighborhood, a ruin now, he resurrects it.

The identity Milosz seizes upon is a curious one. His region was the homeland of "the last pagans of the Western world," the most recent, and therefore most reluctant Christians, tarrying at the edge of Western civilization, as at the edge of their northern forests amid the trolls and *dybbuks* of their still-potent folklore.

He reaches far back, past history and specific data, to a more remote region, perhaps instinctively seeking a source closer to metaphor, an identity that, while carrying the force of ancestry, is not nailed down by calendar history and mere event. *Issa Valley*, his novel which reads like a memoir in its evocation of childhood in Lithuania, uses this pagan folk background liberally; it is more romantic and nostalgic in tone, less powerful than *Native Realm*.

Three effects result from his fastening on the "last pagan" identity as his origin. Allegiance goes first to that early state of national life, of innocence, when good and evil, happiness and grief, body and spirit, are not yet split apart. This pagan innocence bespeaks the guiltless status of small nations, their one victory (ironically, it could be called a *civilized* victory) over the great and dominating nations: They have been spared the spiritually depleting sins of empire. Of course, theirs was not a paradise (Milosz speaks of a history of "recurrent feudalism," a kind of internal colonization). Still:

> While the countries that bordered the Atlantic were acquiring colonies across the seas and setting up manufactures, no such foolhardy ventures interested the Eastern Europeans, who were engaged exclusively in agriculture; and their consciences today are not burdened with the sufferings of black slaves or the first proletarians.

This early identification with the noble savage produced in Milosz "an instinctive loathing for violence disguised as ideology and a skeptical attitude toward the apologetics of all 'civilizers.'" An interesting heritage for the author not only of *Native Realm*, but of *The Captive Mind*, a penetrating study of the appeal of an abstract "system," the working out of an *idea* in postwar Eastern Europe.

Marxism, in its Stalinist-satellite form, is perhaps as far from "parochial loyalty" as one can imagine. "Parochial attachments" are neither theoretical nor even conscious in the way associated with dialectic. They are the adhesions of muscle and bone, the correspondences of kinship. Such attachments are the stuff of indigenous, even regional, culture.

Secondly, his identification with "the last pagans of the Western world" gives Milosz a special relation to his historical Catholicism. He has a nice relish for heresy: "My favorites were the Gnostics, the Manichaeans, and the Albigensians." As a student in a Catholic school, Milosz found great appeal in those heresies that truly gave the Devil his due:

> They at least did not take refuge behind some vague will of God in order to justify cruelty. They called necessity, which

rules everything that exists in time, the work of an evil Demiurge opposed to God. God, separated in this way from the temporal order, subsisted in a sphere proper to himself, free from responsibility, as the object of our desires.

Catholic doctrine, that vast, unbroken ice one skates across in childhood, in adolescence becomes something one must hack through with the very blade of one's faith. As Milosz says, the newfound "bitterness of dualism, the Absolute saved at this price, intoxicated me like the feel of a harsh surface after a smooth one that it is impossible to grasp."

Adolescents are often romantic about evil, even thrilled by it. For Milosz, this flair for a heresy which posits a figure for evil, as God is for good and which allows for the wild card of history, is not simply youthful fascination with the diabolical. This heresy stands for his need to make sense—or perhaps simply to make *something*—of the terrible series of catastrophes visited upon his part of the world and which have come to be known under the heading of the Holocaust. (Milosz insists that the Holocaust must be seen in terms of Europe and of Western civilization, not solely as a Jewish tragedy.)

Of course, all that came later and was not part of his schoolboy angst. But why be dismissive, why call it "schoolboy angst" when Milosz was already worrying about the ancient dilemma of good and evil which our century did not, after all, invent, but has illustrated in exceptionally lurid color.

Finally, this "barbarian" identity that Milosz claims as his original heritage, asserts absolutely the power of the past and the necessity of remembering. If an identity so ancient, so lost to history, still functions, no matter how atavistically, then the past does live and has force. It matters. The mandate is clear: Either we remember the past or the past will have its revenge—will draw us into itself as chaos and destruction, rather than as memory and story.

We embody, if unwittingly and partially, our history, even our prehistory. The past courses through our veins. The self is the instrument which allows us not only to live this truth but to contemplate it, and thereby to be comforted by meaning— which is simply the awareness of relationship. These are difficult notions for the American consciousness to grasp. We have a long habit of creating the self as an expression of the "pursuit of happiness," defined as a changing mass of alternatives which are always imagined to be a private concern for the searching individual.

This last pagan heritage is important for its indications about Milosz's attitude toward a native and proud, "parochial" heritage, and as a source for that boyhood Manichaeism which serves him well as an adult who has lived through appalling times.

But there is another significance to Milosz's cleaving to his pagan heritage: the significance of memory itself. *Native Realm* is not only about Milosz's memories, nor even his nation's. It is about memory. His real quest may be the exploration of the overwhelming power memory has in the face of personal despair (the usual issue for Western memoirists) and brutal outer force (the classic burden of Eastern Europe).

We often say it is necessary to remember in order that "it may never happen again": the terrible It at the heart of the century, and at the center of Europe. As Milosz says in his Nobel Lecture, "the number of books in various languages which deny that the Holocaust ever took place, and claim that it was invented by Jewish propaganda, has exceeded one hundred." The number has grown exponentially since then.

Reason enough to remember. Memory is not just commemoration; it is ethical power. Beyond this, its purpose is not

Similarly, I could say that an underlying quest in my memoir would be the creation of a particular truths — created selves.

simply to edify, nor even to warn, important though that function is. Memory's fundamental instinct is to formulate. That is, to
make a past which is not only accurate (that would be a hopeless task, a naive and misguided enterprise) but *imaginatively*
accurate, as a work of art is. Therefore, no matter how appalling
or tragic its materials, real memory is optimistic, as Milosz says
poetry is, for it creates something:

> Poetry is a constant self-negation; it imitates Heraclitean flu-
> idity. And only poetry is optimistic in the twentieth century,
> through its sensual avidity, its premonitions of change, its
> prophecies with many meanings.

Milosz's first step toward poetry resembles his approach to memoir: the neutralization of the self. We may recognize in Milosz's
poetic manifesto the great testimonial of Keats:

> A Poet is the most unpoetical of any thing in existence;
> because he has no Identity—he is continually in for—and
> filling some other Body—the Sun, the Moon, the Sea and
> Men and Women who are creatures of impulse are poetical
> and have about them an unchangeable attribute—the poet
> has none; no identity. . . . When I am in a room with People
> . . . the identity of everyone in the room begins to press upon
> me that I am in a very little time annihilated. . . .

The self, in other words, becomes instrumental, alert, useful. In
memoir, that use serves memory. Not personal memory, but
memory itself, the tabernacle of human experience.

But with catastrophe there is no desire to remember, and
optimism seems fatuous. When, near the end of *Native Realm*,

Milosz reaches the United States (after the Second World War), he says hopelessly,

> I wanted to forget. In my dreams, fragments would come back to me: a road between the pines above a craggy river bank, a lake with a string of ducks on it; but people above all, uninvited guests, shadows, mostly ordinary men, unintelligent, modestly ambitious, cruelly punished for wanting only to live; various peasants, Jews from ramshackle little towns, a colleague from my high school and university days—a pedant, a plodder, the owner of an idiotic collection of empty cigarette boxes, dreaming of a career as public prosecutor, tortured in some Siberian camp; another, a bald lecher with batlike ears, who told enthusiastically about a garrisoned small town: "We came to Skidel and . . . paradise, I tell you, not a town! Every house a brothel!" They shot him as he stole over the same border I had crossed in 1940; after hearing about it, I could never rid myself of the image of his short, fat fingers clawing at the moss in a death spasm.

He found "the popular legend about America, cut off by an ocean as if by the waters of Lethe, justified." As a diplomatic representative of Poland—"a Red" to jumpy 1950s America, a man who had recently seen Warsaw reduced to nothing, he says he

> walked the streets of Chicago and Los Angeles as if I were an anthropologist privileged to visit the civilizations of Incas or Aztecs. Americans accepted their society as if it had arisen from the very order of nature; so saturated with it were they that they tended to pity the rest of humanity for having

strayed from the norm. If I at least understood that all was not well with me, they did not realize that the opposite disablement affected them: a loss of the sense of history and, therefore, of a sense of the tragic, which is only born of historical experience.

He may have wanted, as he says, to forget. Clearly, he wanted even more to remember—in a new way, if that were possible. This remembering, in its rigorous search, is the work of the imagination, closer to poetry than to fiction, in spite of the apparent narrative affinity of the novel and autobiography, and in spite of the autobiographical nature of much modern fiction. In the lyric poem and the memoir, a self speaks, renders the world, or is recast in its image. In both lyric poetry and the memoir the real subject is consciousness in the light of history. The ability to transmit the impulses of the age, the immediacy of a human life moving through the changing world, is common to both genres. To be personal and impersonal all at once is the goal of both. To be witness, rather than story-teller. The essential human utterance, proper to lyric poetry, comes from the personal voice, the first person. And that same voice, not the particular nature of its story, is also what distinguishes the memoir.

The quest that provides *Native Realm* with its sense of form reveals what quests are always about, even those of war-ravaged, ideology-scarred Eastern Europeans: happiness. Oddly, it is that old historyless American pursuit of happiness. And Milosz claims it:

. . . when I compare us with the inhabitants of calm and orderly countries, I would be inclined, in spite of all our misfortunes and sufferings, to call us happier in one respect. Neither new models of cars, nor travels, nor love affairs provide the elixir of youth. In grabbing our portion of amusements and pleasures, we expose ourselves to the vengeance of time, which dulls receptivity. We Easterners, on the other hand, precisely because we had to gaze into the hells of our century, made the discovery that the elixir of youth is not a delusion. No one brought himself willingly to look into those hells. . . . Nevertheless, it taught us the meaning of full commitment and exploded the barriers between the individual and the social, between style and institution, between aesthetics and politics. The miraculous elixir is nothing other than the certainty that there are no boundaries to the knowledge of what is human. . . .

The elusive self, sought here, there, everywhere, comes to light in the shadowy corridors of history; some measure of peace attends disaster; dislocation provides security; even tragedy gives off a strange radiance. The contraries that bedevil us, that have always sent our civlization on its quests, are held in hand here by this Eastern European poet, regarding his journey through the horrific lens of the century in his bruised region of the world, and through our troubled, if seemingly untouched, American realm.

By the end of his memoir, Milosz seems to have arrived, the point of all quests. This Eastern European has found in his "gaze into the hells of our century" the elixir which the West, in its psychological "probings," thirsts for: a rescue from the melancholy we call anxiety. "I suspect," Milosz writes on the last page of *Native Realm,*

that the individual who lives his journey from childhood to old age against an almost unchanging background, whose habits are never disrupted by the ups and downs of the social order, is too susceptible to the melancholy of things that are simply here, yet are opaque. . . .

Through defeats and disasters, humanity searches for the elixir of youth; that is, of life made into thought, the ardor that upholds belief in the wider usefulness of our individual effort, even if it apparently changes nothing in the iron working of the world. It may be that we Eastern Europeans have been given the head in this search.

He has plucked something untarnished from the smoking heap. He has touched a drop, at least, of that "elixir" the world keeps seeking. And he claims this taste of paradise precisely as one who has seen his world go through hell. It seems strange, this treasure from that terror, this spiritual assurance from utter devastation.

But though Milosz maintains his identity as a "typical Eastern European," he knows the truth the "Eastern" Europeans of our century embody in their experience holds also the missing piece of the West, of our own consciousness, the bitter elixir we quest for too. After all, did we in the West really think that the Grail, once found, would not be filled with blood?

A Book Sealed
with Seven Seals:
Edith Stein

I have no private life anymore, I told myself. All my energy must be devoted to this great happening. Only when the war is over, if I'm still alive then, will I be permitted to think of my private affairs once more.

The year is 1914, summer. Edith Stein is twenty-two, a graduate student in Göttingen, studying philosophy with the phenomenologist Edmund Husserl. In this passage from her autobiography, *Life in a Jewish Family*, she is instructing herself on her place in the First World War, not the Second, though that is the war that finally claimed her and has fixed her in history as one of "the six million."

Yet it is all there already—the stern high-mindedness barely concealing raw passion, the longing to plunge into an existence more commanding than "private life," the urge to be used, even used up, by a consuming reality. There is nothing morbid about it: the innocent grandiosity—"I have no private life anymore," " . . . if I'm still alive"—ripples with excitement. This girl, reading Schopenhauer in her rented room on a July afternoon, when a friend runs in with the news that war has been declared, might just as well have been saying, "At last—I can *live.*"

She says that she slapped shut *The World as Will and Idea* ("Oddly enough, I never took up that particular book again") and headed home to Breslau—not so much because it was home, but because "Göttingen was in the heart of Germany and there was little likelihood it would get to see any of the enemy except possibly prisoners of war. Breslau, on the contrary, was but a few hours' distance from the Russian border and was the most important fortification in the east. That it might soon be besieged by Russian troops was distinctly possible. My decision was made."

The destination she chose was not home, but history. A flight into—what? Thrilling danger? But also into a world, a truth more encompassing than "private life." She wished her own life to be absorbed by a vast plot. The first such grandeur she encountered was the Great War. She ran to it. This was only partly a matter of patriotism (though she and her family were fiercely pro-German, then and much later, so assimiliated that the anti-Semitism of the early National Socialist period struck her mother as implausible, demented, ridiculous). It was clearly Edith Stein's desire to disappear into devotion to a greater good. When a fellow student asked their friend Adolf Reinach, a young philosophy professor at the university, if he too must go to war, Reinach replied, "It's not that I *must;* rather, I'm permitted to go."

"His statement pleased me very much," Edith Stein noted. "It expressed so well my own feelings." What appealed to her was the surrender of individual life to a massive reality encompassing everyone. The self was no good if it was merely personal, merely "personality." Rather, as she wrote in her first book, "The self is the individual's way of structuring experience." The self was necessary—but not for itself. It was necessary as the experiencer of "phenomena," of reality as it is absorbed by a life. Self was meant, in a real sense, to be lost. A kind of blessed anonymity attended the most genuine life, the most realized self.

The desire for anonymity is a desire for greatness. True anonymity, of course, is unconscious, unsought. But the instinct, made conscious, to bury the self's small story in the overwhelming text of history—this is a passion for greatness. In her autobiography, Edith Stein emphasized her "conviction that I was destined for something great." Such greatness should not be confused with mere ambition, for ambition revolves endlessly, and finally hopelessly, around the individual's sense of stardom. Its engine is self-reflexive—whether the ambition looks like arrogance or self-loathing or sheer willfulness.

The urge toward greatness, on the other hand, is oddly aligned with humility. The purpose is not the fulfillment of a self, or its aggrandizement, but the deft insertion of the self into an overwhelming design. Hence, the sensation of "the loss of self." This quest for greatness always carries as well a charge of relation, of service: At the earliest opportunity, Edith Stein rushed, against her mother's strenuous objection, to work as a Red Cross nurse's aid in a camp hospital for soldiers suffering from infectious diseases. Ultimately, a life seeking greatness is about the loss of the self in the service of a more complete reality. It is a disappearing act. It is, sometimes, a martyrdom. That, finally, is how it came to be in the unlikely life of Edith Stein.

*T*his is the plot: A woman, born into a warm German Jewish family, converts to Catholicism several years after she earns her doctorate in philosophy with a brilliant dissertation published under the title *On the Problem of Empathy.* She teaches and lectures at Catholic colleges in German-speaking Europe for a decade. Soon after her teaching career is ended by the Nazi decree against Jewish teachers in 1933, she enters a Carmelite monastery in Cologne and becomes a contemplative nun. After *Kristallnacht,* as conditions worsen in Germany, she is moved to a Carmel in Holland on New Year's Eve, 1938. Three years later, two SS officers raid the Dutch monastery and arrest her. A week after that she is sent in a transport to Auschwitz. She perishes in a gas chamber soon after her arrival there.

That is the life. There is a posthumous existence as well, with its own drama. In 1987 Pope John Paul II beatified Edith Stein as a martyr of the Church in a ceremony in a Cologne stadium, filled with seventy thousand people. Then, in October 1998, the Church took the final step, and canonized Edith Stein in Rome. There has been, not surprisingly, a backlash of protest, mostly from Jewish groups, but also from some chagrined Catholics: What was the Church doing, appropriating as a martyr a woman who, while she died a committed Christian, was murdered precisely because she was Jewish?

Some of Edith Stein's relatives declined to go to the beatification ceremony. But her niece, Susanne Batzdorff, who lives now in California, did attend. Over the years, she has offered sympathetic help to the Carmelite editors and translators of her aunt's work. But as she sat in the stadium that day, she has since written, "Suddenly it hit me: All these people are gathered here to witness my Aunt Edith Stein declared a blessed martyr of the Catholic church. Yet in August 1942, when a freight train carried her to her death in a gas chamber, no one would help or cry out to stop the horror. . . ."

Hers is the inevitable accusation. And interestingly, the question of the propriety of the Church's claiming Edith Stein as a martyr of the Church rests fundamentally on "the problem of empathy," Edith Stein's defining subject. For if the Church cannot see itself as it is reflected by the truth of another suffering population, and if it refuses to acknowledge the judgment of that gaze, then it fails in this essential spiritual exercise of empathy. For the purpose of empathy is the fullness of reality, of truth. "Empathy," Edith Stein wrote, "offers itself to us as a corrective for self-deception." The point of empathy: I allow myself to be seen through the judgment and clarity of your gaze, acknowledging, as Edith Stein says, that "it is possible for another to judge me more accurately than I judge myself and give me clarity about myself." Empathy seeks truth, and along its difficult way, it makes the discovery of compassion as well.

In pursuing Edith Stein's canonization, the Church not only lays itself open to the charge of a troubling insensitivity to Jewish experience, but even more strangely, it denies itself and its people the real benefit of contemplating her death. For if the Church relinquished its claim to her martyrdom, Edith Stein could become for Christians the focal point of an act of contrition still desperately needed by the Western world in response to the midcentury horrors committed against Jews and Jewish life in Christian Europe.

As a Catholic saint, she is folded into the canon of Church history. But where she is needed is exactly where she placed herself: in between. The Catholic Church needs Edith Stein—that's true. Not as a saint of the Church, but as a presence who, against all the odds, stands at the midpoint of the evils of midcentury. She should remain a ghost, a figure calling Christians toward contrition—the proper Christian response to the Holocaust. What would her niece's response have been at a gathering of thousands of Catholics in the Cologne stadium if the occasion had been not a beatification ceremony but a giant open-air act of civic contrition on the part of the Church, extended to Jews living and dead? Catholics must accept the fact that sainthood is not simply a way of honoring a great life; it is inevitably a way of claiming it. The act of contrition must begin with the willingness to relinquish this claim.

Yet this contentious question of Edith Stein's formalization as a martyr of the Church, proper to a discussion of the Church's habits of cultural appropriation, does not belong to Edith Stein. There is a problem, but it is not hers. This ethical question vexes the Church's life, not Edith Stein's. Nor does the question of her canonization belong to any inquiry about her conversion, which was genuine. She kept the reason for her conversion deeply and purposely buried. She remains the riddle containing her seeming contradictions. She, not her "cause" (on either side of the debate), is the fascination. For she is an enigma. That is, she is a life, waiting to be read.

Edith Stein bore a crushing burden of paradox with simplicity, certainty, and humility. She went where she had to go— into the Catholic communion when commanded by faith; then, even deeper, into the cloister of Carmel, and finally, crammed into a fetid boxcar, to Auschwitz. For her, the paradox of her life was not a contradiction to be debated but a truth to be lived. She understood quite early that she would be doubly affected by the crimes of the age as a Christian Jew: "I will always be close to you, to my family, to the Jewish people," she said to her niece, Susanne Batzdorff, when, as a girl, she asked her aunt why she was entering a Christian monastery *now*, just as attacks on Jews were growing. "And don't think my being in a convent is going to keep me immune from what is happening in the world."

If her life is one of the great conundrums of twentieth-century faith, the mystery does not begin when she converted to Roman Catholicism at the age of thirty. She was one born for mystery, it seems, as genius always is. Jan Nota, a Jesuit priest who knew Edith Stein in her final years in the Carmel in Echt, Holland, has written that the "fascinating thing to me about Edith Stein was that truth did not exist as an abstraction for her, but as something incarnated in persons, and therefore as inconceivable apart from love."

From childhood, when she perceived something to be "true," she had to pursue it, do it, be it—whatever it was. She had been a notoriously riotous, unruly child. "I was mercurially lively, always in motion," she writes, "spilling over with pranks, impertinent and precocious, and at the same time, intractably stubborn and angry if anything went against my will. My eldest sister, whom I loved very much, tested her newly-acquired child-training methods on me in vain."

Then, at about the age of seven, she says the "first great transformation took place in me." It was not the result of an external force, she was sure. She could not explain it, she writes in her autobiography, except to say that "reason assumed command within me." She distinctly remembered that "from that time on, I was convinced that my mother and my sister Frieda had a better knowledge of what was good for me than I had; and because of this confidence, I readily obeyed them." Her "old stubbornness" left her. No one could explain the transformation, but for her it was a natural response to an internal recognition: Her behavior changed the instant her perception of "the truth" changed.

Later, the same precise register between perception and

action would draw her into behavior far more flagrant than the childhood furies which once caused her mother such pain. But these changes, so inexplicable and even dismaying to those who loved her, were incontrovertible. Once she seized upon the truth, it claimed her and required action. As a result, she wrote, "I was able to sever the seemingly strongest ties with minimal effort and fly away like a bird escaped from a snare."

But if she could so easily "fly away," she flew alone and into skies darker than her protective family could have imagined. In the midst of an unusually close family, she remained inscrutable. "In spite of the great closeness between us," she wrote, "I couldn't confide in my mother [any] more than in anyone else. From early childhood I led a strange double life that produced alternations of behavior which must have seemed incomprehensible and erratic to any outside observer."

The truth was, she wrote, that within her "another hidden world was emerging, where I would assimilate on my own the things that I saw and heard during the day." She had a naturally heightened sensitivity to suffering as a child, and any observed inequity struck her heart. "Whatever I saw or heard throughout my days was pondered over there"—in her "hidden world." She could not understand how people could laugh at a stumbling, incoherent alcoholic. If anyone spoke of a murder in her presence, she would "lie awake for hours that night, and, in the dark, horror would press in upon me from every corner. . . . I never mentioned a word to anyone of these things which caused me so much hidden suffering. It never occurred to me that one could speak about such matters."

No one else had access to this hidden world, from whence all the "incomprehensible and erratic" behavior came. Her adoring older sisters, already in awe of her grave intelligence and her fierce integrity, despaired of understanding her. So great was her native reserve that they called her, teasing, "the book sealed with seven seals."

*E*dith Stein was born in Breslau, Germany (now Wroclaw, Poland), October 12, 1891, on Yom Kippur, a fact, she always thought, that played into her being her mother's favorite. She was the youngest of seven surviving children out of eleven. Some of her brothers and sisters were nearly adult when she was born. She and her sister Erna, only eighteen months her senior, were the babies, brought up almost as twins.

When Edith was two, her father died suddenly of a heat stroke while he was away on business. Thus began the career of his widow, Auguste Courant Stein, who, against the counsel of her own family, took over the management of her husband's lumber business. The older children helped raise the younger ones, while Auguste kept them all going with her tireless devotion to them and to the business. Against significant odds, she prospered.

A photograph of Auguste, about 1925 (she was seventy-six and would live another eleven years): The stout body, always dressed in black after her husband's death, suggests solidity rather than anything as frivolous as fat. The face is a stone of certainty, not hard but absolute. The jaw is set, the mouth the most telling feature: lips closed in a firm, almost fierce line, giving away nothing. It is not the tense face of a petty domestic dictator, but all the more resolute: a woman used to command, of necessity.

In a facing photograph in *Life in a Jewish Family*, taken at the same time (when she was thirty-four), Edith sits, hand to deep-clefted chin, gazing at the camera neutrally, not feeling required, apparently, to offer any expression. An attractive woman, her mouth surprisingly voluptuous in repose. She is waiting to return to her reading: Her index finger is inserted in the closed book on her lap, marking her place during this brief intrusion.

By the time these two photographs of mother and daughter were made, much had already been decided. Edith, who was a convinced atheist at fifteen in the liberal idealist way her older brothers and sisters had brought to bear in their mother's orthodox home, had eventually come to belief during her university years, probably influenced by the largely Christian—though not Catholic—circle around Husserl. The Master (as Edith and his other devoted students always called him) was Jewish, though he had become a nominal Lutheran, apparently as a professional protection long before Nazi times.

The decisive moment for Edith occured, however, when she was visiting philosopher friends in Bergzabern, during the summer of 1921. One morning, by chance, she picked from a bookshelf a copy of the autobiography of St. Teresa of Avila. Reading it occasioned one of her galvanizing moments of truth. She sat up all night reading. When she put it down the next morning, she said, "This is the truth." She was baptized in the Catholic Church on New Year's Day, 1922.

Auguste was appalled, deeply repelled. "She particularly rejects conversions," Edith wrote to a Catholic friend later. "Everyone ought to live and die in the faith in which they were born. She imagines atrocious things about Catholicism and life in a convent." Going off, against her mother's wishes, to serve in a *lazaretto* during the war had been one thing, but this was a bizarre infatuation, a monstrous disloyalty.

Worse was to come. On October 15, 1933, three days after her forty-second birthday (on the feast day of Teresa of Avila), Edith Stein entered the Carmelite monastery of Cologne as a postulant. Her conversion to Catholicism and her conviction of her vocation to Carmel had come virtually together. Before her baptism, she "still cherished," she says, " . . . the dream of a great love and of a happy marriage." Earlier, there had been a fondness (apparently chaste) between Edith and a fellow philosophy student, Hans Lipps. But she was never willing to sacrifice her profession to marriage. Later, after Lipps married and had two small children and his wife suddenly died, he approached Edith Stein again. "Too late," she is reported to have said. But this was not the romantic "too late" of disappointed dreams, but quite simply, the acknowledgment that she was already committed: By then she was baptized, and with her conversion came her vocation to Carmel.

The eleven-year wait between baptism and entrance into the monastery was largely a form of obedience to her spiritual advisers. They cautioned against hasty action on the part of enthusiastic converts. No doubt they also felt Edith's talents as lecturer and teacher had a place in the world. She was willing to be guided in this, and was a diligent intellectual worker, turning her philosophical gift now toward Thomas of Aquinas, writing and lecturing to Catholic audiences about medieval mysticism and the place of women in the world and in the Church. Her writing of the period is lucid, sensible, progressive (she makes a cogent case for sex education in the schools, for example, and argues with prescience about the importance of a wider role for women in religion).

There was another reason to wait. She admitted that at first she had thought of her baptism as "preparation for entrance into the [Carmelite] Order." But several months later, seeing her mother for the first time since her baptism she realized that Auguste "couldn't handle another blow for the present. Not that it would have killed her—but I couldn't have held myself responsible for the embitterment it would have caused."

Before her conversion, she had tried to follow her brilliant *summa* doctorate with a regular university appointment, but the rigidly hierarchical German academic system was not ready for a woman. No one was willing to sponsor her *habilitation*, the necessary second thesis required for university appointment. The fervent feminism she championed in her youth met the hard wall of habit and entrenched power. She spent her professional career at Catholic colleges, and became a much-sought-after lecturer in Germany, Austria, and Switzerland, in particular.

But clearly, already by 1922, she knew she was a contemplative nun. She lived in a room adjacent to the nuns' quarters at the college where she taught, and attended daily Mass, following the daily prayers of the Divine Office. In effect, she managed to mimic a monastic life years before her entrance into Carmel.

*W*hen Edith Stein was asked to reveal the nature of her religious conversion, she refused. There is no essay or memoir, not even a letter to a trusted friend—nothing—that sheds light on what exactly caused her decisive action. We know that she read Teresa of Avila and recognized there "the truth." And so she followed it. This had been her pattern since her "first transformation" when she was a willful seven-year-old and suddenly, inexplicably, felt that "reason assumed command" within her. Now it was not her mother and her older sister who "had a better knowledge of what was good" for her. Now it was the Holy Spirit itself.

What she found in Teresa she also kept to herself, though certainly she is not the first person to have been profoundly affected by that ardent personality. Even today, almost four and a half centuries since she wrote it, Teresa's autobiography remains one of the most vivid personal documents in the history of Christian testimony, at least as spirited as Saint Augustine's *Confessions*, and more charming. These three—Augustine, Teresa, Edith—form a fascinating linked chain of conversions, each in turn liberated from what Teresa calls in her autobiography, "the shadow of death," which left them utterly worn out with interior struggle.

As Waltraud Herbstrith, one of Edith Stein's biographers, notes, the three "shadows" were different for each of them, but the sense of liberation was the same: For Augustine the snare was unbridled sensuality, for Teresa the surface pleasures of "society" and its tendency to skim over life, lightly. For Edith Stein, it was the twentieth-century existential burden: a rationalist, materialist world view which did not permit the freedom to offer oneself to God. From carnality, to society's distractions, to cold intellectualism: These three figures are cameos of Western civilization's history of spiritual dilemmas.

Edith Stein's reticence about her conversion is striking even in this context of Catholic memoir. It sets her apart from Augustine and from Teresa, for her autobiography does not touch on Christian themes, whereas Augustine and Teresa tremble with the news. Edith Stein's silence bears the particular stamp of her faith—and of her solidarity with her Jewishness. There is nothing "apostolic" about Edith Stein, not a whiff of evangelism pervades her writing. She has no desire to convince anyone of anything—not to persuade and absolutely not to convert. What had happened to her, what continued to happen to her thanks to the daily grace of liturgical and contemplative prayer, was a mystery. It was simply to be lived.

That was not only enough, it was hard enough. It is often difficult to understand what "contemplative life" is about—or for. But Edith Stein was entering this hidden world (literally, an "enclosure") against a backdrop of incomprehension and even antagonism from her family and professional friends. What on earth was she doing this for? Her mother, appalled by her daughter's conversion, cried in frustration, "Why did you have to get to know him? He was a good man—I'm not saying anything against him. But why did he have to go and make himself God?"

In fact, it was the full-time occupation of prayer that sent Edith Stein to Carmel. What is often overlooked, especially in recent times, about the Catholic tradition is that, in spite of its glaring refusals and inequities regarding women, it remains the only Western tradition which has an unbroken history of providing a respected way of life for women outside the domestic roles of wife and mother. The work of a nun and of a monk is identical; it is the *opus Dei*, the work of God, to pray, specifically, to pray without ceasing. If this was the call, then Edith Stein must go where that was the business of each day. Such faith had nothing to do either with dogma or with convincing other people of anything. In addition, the choice of Carmel is telling. Edith Stein chose the one Catholic contemplative order whose roots extend past Christianity back into the hermetic tradition of the Old Testament. Carmelites, though they take their rule from Teresa and much of their tradition of contemplative practice from John of the Cross, look back to Elijah as the first "Carmelite."

Perhaps the most striking example of Edith Stein's unwillingness to meddle in the spiritual lives of others (which in her case contains the converse: her absolute commitment to following her own conviction, against all inducements otherwise) concerns Edmund Husserl, her revered Master. Though he did not die until 1938, five years after Edith entered the Cologne Carmel, he was already pondering his death and considering religious as well as philosophical questions in 1930 when, in

February, Edith wrote an important letter to a mutual friend about him.

Edith was living at the time with the Dominican nuns at St. Magdalena college at Speyer where she taught literature and history; Husserl was in Freiburg, retired but still writing. They rarely saw each other, and the intimate teacher-student relationship was a thing of the fond Göttingen past. The friend to whom she wrote, a Benedictine nun named Sister Adelgundis Jaegerschmid, was living in Freiburg, and so had access to Husserl there. Edith's letter is a response to Sister Adelgundis's mention of a conversation with the Master in which she had managed (she felt) to nudge him along the path of considering "the last things" (in Catholic doctrine: death, judgment, heaven, and hell).

Edith is clearly alarmed by this intrusion into the old man's spiritual process. "I believe one must be on one's guard against illusions," she writes back (immediately) to Sister Adelgundis. "It is good to be able to speak to him so freely about the last things. But doing so heightens his responsibility as well as *our* responsibility for him. Prayer and sacrifice are surely more important than anything we can say to him. . . ."

She goes on to make a broader association, distinct from her concern about Husserl: "There is a real difference between being a chosen instrument and being in a state of grace. It is not up to us to pass judgment, and we may confidently leave all to God's unfathomable mercy. But we may not becloud the importance of these last things. After every encounter in which I am made aware how powerless we are to exercise direct influence, I have a deeper sense of the urgency of my own *holocaustum*."

It is eerie, of course, to see that word—*holocaust*—employed here, almost as if it were a prophetically macabre job description Edith Stein had written for herself. It would be a mistake to make too much of it. But neither should it be passed over as simply a coincidence, haunting but without significance. For Edith Stein clearly understood—as mystics of all faiths and "ways" do—that the end point of contemplative life is the oneness which unites the individual with the fullest reality. With God, yes. And with the suffering world as well. The same conviction caused Buddhist monks to incinerate themselves on the streets of Saigon and before the United Nations in New York during the Vietnam War. They too understood, literally, that their own sacrifice would unite evil and its helpless victims in a liberating instant. Redemption requires that radical evil and radical atonement collide. Edith Stein was irresistibly drawn to this collision. As she had been drawn to the earlier conflagration of the First World War when she declared as a passionate university student, "I have no private life anymore." She was still trying to "lose her life," now in a frankly religious sense.

Which is not to say she longed for death or imagined foolishly that she could change anything. She cautions that even to *speak* to another, to evangelize as her Benedictine friend so naively reports doing, is a misguided action, dangerous even, spiritually and personally for both sides of the equation. She felt such discussion jeopardized the root enterprise of active faith, the personal atonement which every day she saw grew more necessary as the evil took hold of Germany.

As the political situation in Germany worsened for Jews, her focus on sacrifice grew. "Though she never complained outwardly," one of her students reported later to Waltraud Herbstrith, "nevertheless it was heartrending to have to see her gentle face contorted in pain. . . . I can still hear her saying, 'One day this will all have to be atoned for.'"

The silence she felt was incumbent on her has made her, strangely enough, a peculiarly contemporary believer: one whose respect for the range of beliefs (and disbeliefs) is so strong that "proofs" seem childish. Only the living, incontrovertible experience itself, mystical and unbidden and therefore unspeakable, will do. The contemporary believer, even one wrapped in the mantle of the established Church, living within a cloister, must give witness in a culture of disbelief, in a secular and, in her case, lawless culture.

This silence did not extend to the repression of her own protest against what was happening, however. Before entering the Cologne Carmel, she wrote—twice, apparently—to Pius XI, requesting an audience to discuss the plight of the Jews, urging him to make a strong statement against this lawlessness. He denied her request for an audience, and sent her in reply a papal blessing. Pius XI was very sick at the time, which perhaps mitigates somewhat how history regards this incident. He died soon afterward, and was followed by Pius XII, the Pope who reigned during the Second World War.

One more thing about Edith Stein's sense of her own sacrifice. It is significant that she used the Latin word—*holocaustum*—and not the vernacular. She was a brilliant Latin scholar, and had always been drawn to the language from her first study of it. Her use of Latin here and elsewhere is not the flourish of an intellectual fop. In *Life in a Jewish Family*, she says she felt, when she began studying Latin, "it was as though I were learning my mother tongue." This was long before she prayed in Latin or thought of it as the language of the Church. Just as the precision of Bach and his elegant resolution of great complexities made him her favorite composer, so it was that of all her languages (and she was a gifted linguist, easily adding Greek and English, French, and Dutch, as she went through life), Latin was the tongue that best suited her.

In her autobiography and in the letters, it is clear that when her passion quickens at the edge of the inexpressible, she resorts instinctively to Latin and its crisp, minimalist beauty. It was not, for her, a brittle, lost language, but the supreme mode of taut expression. Her most intimate revelations revert to Latin, as if there she could be relieved, finally, of the burden of her meaning. And so it is no surprise that when her closest philosopher friend, Hattie Conrad-Martius, asked her the question that every reader now asks: *What caused your conversion?*—Edith Stein replied, *Secretum meum mihi*, my secret is mine (literally "my secret to me").

Josephine Koeppel, the splendid and meticulous English translator of the autobiography and letters, calls this an "amazingly abrupt" response, and yet it is the right one for the new, converted Edith. The great Teresa herself, Koeppel notes, encouraged her nuns "to talk together about spiritual subjects in general, but she frowned on making a display out of one's prayer, or of 'the secrets of the King.'"

Edith Stein, the book her family said was "sealed with seven seals" even when she was a child, remained loyal to mystery, and spoke of herself only to the limit of usefulness. The rest, she knew, belonged to her future, her *holocaustum*. It was, in any case, as she said to her closest friend, *secretum meum mihi*.

And what, finally, of the *holocaustum*? Especially the Jewish anguish she saw firing all around her, the anguish which she knew would claim her too. What did this do to her Christian conviction? Where did her solidarity lie? And did she understand her life was a martyrdom?

Everything suggests that Edith Stein was an unusually integrated person, capable of a high state of contemplative prayer. It seems clear that she adapted naturally to the core of prayer: She understood her vocation as an act of solidarity (or, her old word, empathy) with the suffering of the world. She chose for her name in Carmel, Sister Teresa Benedicta of the Cross. The Cross was where she stood. Of all the Christian mysteries—the incarnation, the resurrection—none magnetized her as the cross did. It was *her* mystery, and she made it her name. It was not for her an empty or merely edifying metaphor, but the image of shared, and ultimately redemptive, pain.

Yet in her most telling book, *Life in a Jewish Family,* she does not touch on Christian imagery, on her conversion, or on the story of her struggle. The book covers the years from her birth in 1891 (with backward looks at earlier family history) until 1916, that is, it covers the period before her conversion. But that does not in itself explain the absence of Christian reference, for she was obviously writing it from the standpoint of a Christian life (indeed, she wrote most of it in Carmel and began it at the insistence of a Jesuit friend).

The history of the book's composition is instructive: In January 1933, the Nazis seized power in Germany. Within a few weeks, Edith Stein, like all Jewish teachers, lost her job. She left Münster where she had recently taken a position, and returned home to Breslau. There, during the next six months, she wrote the first part of the book. She felt "the new dictators" of Germany had so caricatured Jewish life, that many Germans, especially younger people, "being reared in racial hatred from earliest childhood," had no idea of the truth. To all who had been thus deprived of the truth, "we who grew up in Judaism have an obligation to give our testimony."

Nowhere in Edith Stein's writing is there the troubling distaste for Judaism and Jewish life that sometimes betrays itself in Simone Weil's work. For Edith Stein, Judaism (and more to the point, Jews) are not subject to judgment. They *are*—and are human. Therefore, to be honored in their persons and in their beliefs. And of course, treasured in her own personal life and memory.

In October 1933, when she entered Carmel, she took up the work of the autobiography again almost immediately, and wrote the majority of the text in the next eighteen months in the Cologne novitiate.

A strange project for a postulant to undertake, at her superiors' urging, as her first work in a Carmelite monastery, this detailed memoir of a Jewish upbringing. But her faithfulness to her specifically Jewish identity precluded any diversion from the task she saw as another strict part of her calling: the representation of a real Jewish family to an ignorant (she wished) and hostile (she knew) audience.

She never completed the book, though she tried to return to it. But circumstances intervened. And in an effort to find safety for herself and also for her community, she requested to be transferred to a Carmel in Palestine. Too late. The British had already closed that escape route. In the end, she moved to the Carmel in Echt, arriving New Year's Day, 1939, aware that she was also transferring to the Dutch monastery the very risk she had brought into the Cologne enclosure. It was impossible for her, carrying Jewish identity papers, to bring the manuscript of *Life in a Jewish Family* across the border. But once in Echt, she asked if someone could be found to bring the manuscript from Germany into Holland. A young Marianhill missionary, named Father Rhabanus, volunteered. At the border, the police searched his car and picked up the bulky manuscript, flipping through the pages idly. "Your doctoral thesis, evidently," the policeman said, and tossed it back in the car, letting him pass through.

Time was running out. Edith Stein wrote only a few pages before the Nazis invaded and occupied Holland. The manuscript had again become a fearful liability. If it was found in a Nazi search (and monasteries were suspect places), the book would put the entire community at risk. At one point, she buried it on the monastery grounds. Then, fearful of the effects of moisture on her carefully wrapped package, she dug it up again and had a sister hide it elsewhere. It caused her much worry; she was troubled, as well, that her presence jeopardized her community. She also had another pressing project under way: She desperately wished to complete *The Science of the Cross*, her study of John of the Cross, in time for the four-hundred-year anniversary of the father of Carmel in 1942.

She and her superiors began a search for a new sanctuary for her. They were working feverishly on efforts to remove her (and her older sister Rosa, who had also converted to Catholicism and was sheltering at the Echt monastery as a refugee) to a Carmel in Switzerland. Then, on Sunday, July 26, 1942, over three years after her arrival in Echt, a pastoral letter from the Dutch bishops was read in all Catholic churches, denouncing the Nazi policies toward the Jews.

The next day, "because the Bishops interfered," Reichskommissar Seyss-Inquart ordered all Catholic Jews to be deported before week's end. The official Nazi memorandum listed 722 Jews registered as Catholics throughout the country. A further memorandum, dated July 31, claimed that four thousand Jews registered as Christians had been gathered in one camp. This information was seen as a threat to induce the bishops to stop their protest of the general deportations.

On August 2, 1942, at 5:00 P.M., after Edith Stein (Sister Benedicta) had, as was the custom, read the point of meditation, the evening hour of mental prayer began. The silence was interrupted several minutes later by loud pounding on the door which echoed into the nuns' choir. The S.S. had arrived. Before the nuns realized what was happening, Edith Stein and her sister Rosa were being taken away.

Rosa, terrified, at first became hysterical. Her younger sister turned to go, and gently told her to follow. "Come," Edith said to Rosa, "let us go for our people."

Not "to our people," but "for" them. Her *holocaustum* had begun.

They were taken to the transfer camp at Westerbork, from which all Dutch Jews (including, two years later, Anne Frank) were sent east. They were with other Catholics, some of them also nuns and priests. On August 6, from Barracks 36 at Westerbork, Edith sent a card to the Echt Carmel, requesting a few necessary items: "woolen stockings, two blankets. For Rosa all the warm underwear and whatever was in the laundry; for us both towels and wash cloths. Rosa also has no toothbrush, no Cross and no rosary." Then, strangely radiant, "so far I have been able to pray, gloriously."

It was her last written communication. There was a brief, false, hope of release or "deferments" for these Catholic Jews. Then came news that all such releases were revoked. An Ursuline nun (also a Jewish convert) wrote later of observing Edith Stein when she received this news: "I saw the German Carmelite. Her release had also been cancelled. Pale but composed, she kept on comforting her fellow-sufferers."

A few days later when a group of men, sent from the Echt Carmel, managed to visit the prisoners in Westerbork, they reported that Edith related everything "in a calm and quiet manner." They had been smoking as she spoke, "and after she finished, in the hope of relieving the tension a little, we jokingly offered her a cigarette. That made her laugh. She told us that back in her days as a university student she had done her share of smoking, and dancing too." They were surprised by her "lighthearted happiness." Later, when the S.S. patrol signaled the prisoners back into their barracks with a harsh whistle, Edith said, "I am prepared for whatever happens." Apparently, she expected to be sent to a forced labor camp in her native Silesia, to work in the mines.

On August 7, 1942, she and Rosa, along with many of their fellow prisoners, were conveyed by cattle car from Westerbork toward the east.

Final sightings: In 1948 the Prioress of the Cologne Carmel writes that in August 1942, Valentin Fouquet, the stationmaster in the town of Schifferstadt, reported that he heard himself called from the transport that had stopped briefly in the station. A "lady in dark clothes," who said her name was Stein, asked him to tell her friends that she sent greetings and was on her way to Poland.

Then, in 1982, a man named Johannes Wieners published a piece claiming that on August 7, 1942, he had spoken with Edith Stein. There is no proof, only his testimony. He had been working as a postal driver and was assigned to an army post office in Breslau. A freight train came in on the track alongside his and halted. The guard opened the sliding door, and he could see people penned up, "listlessly squatting on the floor. There was a horrible strench coming from the car."

A woman who was dressed in a nun's habit came to the door. "I guess because I looked sympathetic to her, she said to me, 'It's terrible. We don't even have containers to relieve ourselves.' After that, she looked into the distance at Breslau and said, 'This is my home; I'll never see it again.'"

Wieners says he stared at her, and then she said, "We are going to our death."

"That really shook me," Wieners wrote. "I remember that I asked her, 'Do the other prisoners know about this?' She answered very slowly, 'It's better for them not to know.'"

An engine was hooked up to his mail train then, and it

pulled out, headed also toward Poland. "But when I got back from internment in 1948," he says, "I read about Edith Stein in a magazine. The minute I saw the picture, I knew it was the sister from August 7, 1942."

That is all there is. Maybe—because the account by Johannes Wieners has no corroboration—it is more than there is. On June 2, 1958, the Bureau of Information of the Netherlands Red Cross sent the nuns in Echt and Cologne a final certification concerning Edith Stein, with information dated February 15, 1950:

FOR REASONS OF RACE AND SPECIFICALLY BECAUSE OF JEWISH DESCENT

On 2 August, 1942 ARRESTED in Echt.

On 5 August, 1942, HANDED OVER in K.L. Westerbork and

On 7 August, 1942, DEPORTED from K.L. Westerbork to K.L. Auschwitz.

THE ABOVE NAMED PERSON IS TO BE CONSIDERED AS HAVING DIED ON 9 August, 1942 in AUSCHWITZ.

The mind goes back instinctively to the brief flashes that spark from Edith Stein's memoir as if to live again in her life rather than her death, jots of personal life indelibly inscribed in her account of her "life in a Jewish family." They are the small moments she chose to rescue and reveal as evidence of simple humanity—family parties, mountain hikes with her student friends, as idyllic as scenes out of a German operetta ("No one growing up during or since the [First World] war can possibly imagine the security in which we assumed ourselves to be living before 1914"), dances and jokes, the heated arguments and reconciliations of young intellectuals, the months at the *lazaretto*, seeing physical suffering and desperation as she never had before, the intensity of her philosophical inquiry, the thrilling proximity to Husserl.

Taking the whole of Edith Stein's life into mind, it is impossible not to see this memoir as part of her sacrifice as well. She is offering up the enormous fact of her family's reality, its appeal, its humanity, to the hostile gaze of a world lit by racial hatred. The Greek root of the word *martyr* is often invoked: It means to witness. But in a deeper recess of the word's etymology there is also a related Sanskrit derivation—from *smar*, to remember. A fierce act of memory then—the will to remember—is the hidden kernel of the martyr's calling. And naturally, the martyr's literary form would be the memoir.

The strangely instinctive solitude of this woman even as a girl is threaded through this family history. Even when she was quite young, she radiated the dignity of her "hidden world," when she first encountered the edge of death by accident one morning when the flame went out in the gas jet of the bedroom she and her sister Erna shared. They lay in their beds, "deathly white, . . . in a heavy stupor." When her sister Frieda discovered them, and opened the windows, letting fresh air rush into the room, Edith "returned to consciousness out of a state of sweet, dreamless rest." To her surprise, she says, "what flashed through my mind upon coming to and grasping the situation was the thought: What a shame! Why couldn't they leave me in this deep peace forever? I myself was shocked to discover that I 'clung to life' so little."

She clung, finally, to something firmer than life. But what is the name of that thing? Was it revelation she found at the foot of the Cross? Or the redemptive value of suffering that sustained her? Did she really smile, and move through Westerbork "like an angel," as the reports say, playing with the children, helping to knit up the shreds of courage torn from the adults? Did she appear at the cattle car door, did she know she was heading to her death?

It is gone now with her into the gray midcentury smoke she became. How it all happened, what it meant to her, how she understood it—these are hidden away with the mystery of her conversion which, as she told Hattie Conrad-Matius, she kept as the *secretum meum mihi*, refusing to divulge, even to her best friend, what she knew each person must find alone, in the locked tabernacle of the self.

The Smile of Accomplishment: Sylvia Plath's Ambition

November 1966, and before me is a book titled *Ariel* which I am reviewing for the University of Minnesota student newspaper. It is the first book review I've ever written. I push on, past my timidity, with a lead I hope is punchy: "Women poets, as a rule, have a hard time of it."

I am the only girl on the student literary magazine. I am not really aware that I'm the only girl on the staff; I don't see things that way yet. It would never occur to me to say I am the only *woman* on staff. I want to be a writer, and I bring more urgency to this desire than to anything I actually want to write about.

That, roughly, was the situation when I asked to review *Ariel* in the fall of 1966. I had to do some fast talking to get the literary editor's permission. "Who's Sylvia Plath?" he said. "I can't see giving her any inches." Copy was measured in column inches.

"She committed suicide," I said, in an attempt to boost her reputation. He was convinced finally when he saw that a famous poet, Robert Lowell, had written an introduction to the book in which he called the poems a "triumph."

I hold now the elderly, fragile newsprint of my review. What in the world was I thinking when I wrote this oddly chipper prose? I note approvingly that Plath "is no crusader." I compliment her for being "well past movements, improvements, or a better deal for the little woman intellectual." Rather, I say, Sylvia Plath "is trying to survive." I don't explain what I mean by surviving. I speak airily of Plath's "brand of femininity," which I say is composed of "concerns more basic to woman than the traditional feminine hang-ups of babies and repressed sexuality." I don't explain what is more basic than sexuality and babies. Nor do I seem to think it strange to refer to babies as a hang-up.

I don't remember writing the review. But I do remember *reading* it in the student union as soon as the paper came out Friday morning. The boldface Bodoni headline cut deeply into the unmarked surface of my ambition:

PLATH WRITES NASTY, BITTER, COMPELLING POETRY

Below the headline, a little smaller but just as boldly inky, was my byline. Then the inches and inches of words. My words. That's what I remember. That's what it was all about: I had managed to get published.

*I*t is hard to think of a poet, certainly any woman poet, who has documented an ambition as ferocious as Sylvia Plath's. Her relationship with *The New Yorker*, faithfully logged in her journal, was positively operatic:

> . . . My baby "The Matisse Chapel," which I have been spending the imaginary money from and discussing with modest egoism, was rejected by *The New Yorker* this morning with not so much as a pencil scratch on the black-and-white doom of the printed rejection. I hid it under a pile of papers like a stillborn illegitimate baby. . . .

She entered contests, sent off poems and stories dutifully in her SASEs. She raged and wept and castigated herself over rejections, then rose again to stuff fresh envelopes for other magazines, other contests.

As everyone knows, she sometimes prevailed. Before she left Smith, she was a literary figure on campus; she had published a prize-winning story in *Mademoiselle*, seven poems in *Seventeen,* and had won prizes for her poetry. She even received letters from admiring fans:

> Hundreds of dreaming ambitious girls would like to be in my place. They write me letters, asking if they may correspond with me.

She seems bewildered that this success, along with "a few lovely clothes, and one intelligent, handsome boy," has not satisfied her.

In the very next paragraph of her journal, she turns to the ominous question:

> Why did Virginia Woolf commit suicide? Or Sara Teasdale or the other brilliant women? Neurotic? Was their writing sublimation (oh, horrible word) of deep, basic desires? If only I

knew. If only I knew how high I could set my goals, my
requirements for my life!

The assumption behind the question seems to be that, for a
woman, the inner urge to accomplishment is not one of the
"deep, basic desires" of life. Ambition is the shameful desire of an
aberrant—because selfish—female life.

There is a breathless, fevered quality to Plath's ambition, as if
the stillborn illegitimate baby she must hide is not a poem
rejected by *The New Yorker* but the private impulse that gave rise
to the writing of the poem in the first place. Even her discipline
troubles her; it is not a good habit, but an addiction. "Why am I
obsessed," she writes in her 1951 journal, the summer before her
sophomore year, "with the idea I can justify myself by getting
manuscripts published?"

Plath suffered from crushing attacks of jealousy as well.
Ambition at least was something she could call discipline; it was
work. Jealousy, on the other hand, was a blight; it spread everywhere, seeping out of the bounds of literary or academic com-
petition into the very fabric of her self:

I am jealous of those who think more deeply, who write
better, who draw better, who ski better, who look better,
who love better, who live better than I. . . .

This pattern doesn't shift until she marries Ted Hughes. Then, for
all the joy she expresses in finding a partner, the heavy plot only
thickens: She becomes ambitious for two.

In the early girlhood journal entries she is crazed by her
ambition, plagued by jealousy and scorekeeping. She is aware
that her seriousness cuts her off from something else she craves:

social life leading to intimacy. The experience of being a college grind is so painful she writes of it in her journal in the literary second person:

> There comes a time when you walk downstairs to pick up a letter you forgot, and the low confidential voices of the little group of girls in the living room suddenly ravels into an incoherent mumble and their eyes slide slimily through you, around you, away from you in a snaky effort not to meet the tentative half-fear quivering in your own eyes. . . . You know it was meant for you, so do they who stab you. . . . So you hear her say to you, "we'd rather flunk school and be sociable than stick in our rooms all the time," and very sweetly, "I never see you. You're always studying in your room!" And you keep your mouth shut. And oh, how you smile!

After her marriage, this changes. "And here I am," she exults in the journal, "Mrs. Hughes. And wife of a published poet." The humiliating loneliness of the scholarship girl has been companioned: She is Mrs. Hughes. And the ferocious ambition has been assuaged by projection: She is married to a published poet.

Plath's ambition, which had been a shameful passion precisely because it was "selfish," seemed more acceptable to her now. The attacks of jealousy are bleached away in the light of marriage, replaced by the happy fretfulness of a devoted wife:

> . . . woke . . . depressed over Ted's 3 rejections of poems from *The Nation* (after 3 acceptances in a row, a stupid letter from M. L. Rosenthal, rejecting them for the wrong reasons). . . . Ted is an excellent poet: full of blood & discipline, like Yeats. Only why won't these editors see it???

When Ted Hughes's first book, *The Hawk in the Rain*, is accepted for publication in 1957, Plath's delight is touchingly absolute:

> I am so glad Ted is first. All my pat theories against marrying a writer dissolve with Ted: his rejections more than double my sorrow & his acceptances rejoice me more than mine. . . .

It is heartbreaking to read such guilelessness from a person who in her earlier journal is a barracuda about her career, a woman whose ambition seemed her bosom companion. But for once we, her posthumous readers, are more ironic than she: Ah yes, his rejections more than double your sorrow. The post-feminist eyebrow arches.

Through it all—college, marriage, babies, end of marriage— Plath kept writing. She remained steely about her discipline and steadfast about the value of publishing. "Being born a woman," she writes in her early college journal, "is my awful tragedy." That is, a tragedy for her ambition.

*W*hen I was reviewing *Ariel* in 1966, Sylvia Plath's suicide struck me as inexplicable. A few years later, with the articulation of early feminist criticism, that suicide was so highly explicated it had become an archetype. It almost ceased to be the real death of an actual person; Plath's suicide "stood" for an unbearable inequity suffered by generations of women artists. Thus began her brief career as a feminist saint, as victim/martyr.

By 1970 it was already possible to read a great deal *about* Sylvia Plath. But her suicide did not speak to me; it remained a melodramatic finish to the real story. For the real story, to me, was the exemplary tale of her ambition. She was a woman who had not been afraid or ashamed to *try*.

She made ambition seem less wrong for a woman. I saw her ambition in wholly sociological terms and was cheered by it. I did not consider the psychological cost of her struggle.

My own early heroine-hunting had been all about seeking the model of the serious girl writer who prevailed. I deleted Plath's suicide, and put in boldface her strenuous discipline and all those self-addressed manila envelopes stuffed with poems sent to big magazines. Feminism latched on to Plath as a figure of the thwart-ed woman; I held on to her as an exemplary apprentice writer.

But now it seems to me that just as her victim/martyr role has since been dismantled, thereby liberating her poetry, so too her consuming ambition no longer seems "feminist." Her jour-nals, in particular, show that this seething ambition was not merely a model of careerism. Her fever pitch, in fact, was not fundamentally about literature. Plath's was a religious hunger which never got the name it deserved: It was a spiritual, not a lit-erary, quest.

Plath wrote most of the *Ariel* poems in the fall of 1962, just after the breakup of her marriage. On October 16, 1962, exact-ly in the middle of the *Ariel* month (thirty poems in that single month), she wrote her mother, "I am a genius of a writer; I have it in me. I am writing the best poems of my life; they will make my name. . . . " No one else had yet seen any of the poems.

This statement to her mother is reminiscent of Keats's famous remark in a letter to his brother and sister-in-law in 1818: "I think I shall be among the English Poets after my death." Keats had his *annus mirabilis* (1818–19), as Plath had her miraculous autumn of 1962. Though Plath's genius is notorious-ly self-absorbed and Keats's is unusually unself-conscious, they belong in some ways to the same tribe.

The summer of 1951, when she had a baby-sitting job for a family in Swampscott, Massachusetts (she was nineteen), Plath wrote this luminous passage in her journal after a hike by the ocean:

> A serene sense of the slow inevitability of the gradual changes in the earth's crust comes over me. A consuming love, not of a god, but of the clean unbroken sense that the rocks which are nameless, the waves which are nameless, the ragged grass which is nameless, are all defined momentarily through the consciousness of the being who observes them. With the sun burning into rock, and flesh, and the wind ruffling grass and hair, there is an awareness that the blind immense unconscious impersonal and neutral forces will endure, and that the fragile, miraculously knit organism which interprets them, endows them with meaning, will move about for a little, then falter, fail, and decompose at last into the anonymous soil, voiceless, faceless, without identity.

Though the word is not used in this passage, the subject clearly is the poet's mission. This powerfully serene voice is not the one usually associated with Sylvia Plath. It is very Keatsian in its radiance. His letter to his brother and sister-in-law in Kentucky comes to mind:

> The mighty abstract Idea I have of Beauty in all things stifles the more divided and minute domestic happiness . . . , but I must have a thousand of those beautiful particles to fill up my heart. I feel more and more every day, as my imagination strengthens, that I do not live in this world alone but in a thousand worlds—No sooner am I alone than shapes of epic greatness are stationed around me. . . .

The reverence, both in the passage from Plath's journal and in Keats's letter, emanates from a direct sensation of poetry experienced in nature. For Keats, the relation was as intense and fundamental as family: "The roaring of the wind is my wife and the Stars through the window pane are my Children," he says elsewhere.

The reverence for other writers and their accomplishments is, for Plath as it was also for Keats, sometimes a thrilling goad, sometimes an invitation to masochistic self-criticism. As Plath says in an early journal entry:

> I am closest to Amy Lowell, in actuality, I think. I love the lyric clarity and purity of Elinor Wylie, the whimsical, lyrical, typographically eccentric verse of E.E. Cummings, and yearn toward T.S. Eliot, Archibald MacLeish, Conrad Aiken. . . . And when I read, God, when I read the taut, spare, lucid prose of Louis Untermeyer, and the distilled intensities of poet after poet, I feel stifled, weak, pallid, mealy-mouthed and utterly absurd.

In his biography of Keats, W. Jackson Bate addresses the issue of fame and the young genius-poet's positive need for models of greatness. He refers to Whitehead's remark that "moral education is impossible apart from the habitual vision of greatness." This is so, Bate says, because "the ideal of greatness, as the Greeks discovered, is ultimately self-corrective in its effect as well as self-impelling."

The *ideal* of greatness—not the evidence or even the example of greatness. But of course the ideal imposes the search for the actual. It sometimes caused Sylvia Plath to light her taper before rather unlikely icons ("the taut, spare lucid prose of Louis Untermeyer?"), just as the very young Keats felt an initial reverence for Leigh Hunt's poetry which he later recognized was inflated.

Plath's ambition was a thirst for greatness, and also a private, curiously humble recognition of her call to be "the fragile, miraculously knit organism which interprets" that she understood to be the poet's true identity. "Yes, God," she says in the same Swampscott journal entry, "I want to talk to everybody I can as deeply as I can. I want to be able to sleep in an open field, to travel west, to walk freely at night."

For a woman, a girl of nineteen, to wish to "walk freely at night," is a poignant wish, of course. Hardly less poignant than her perfect definition of the poet—a person who wishes to talk to everybody as deeply as possible. Her vision here is as incandescent and winning as Emily Dickinson's desire to write a "letter to the world that never wrote to me." In a later journal entry, Plath echoes Dickinson directly, wondering whether she has "the ability or genius to write a big letter to the world. . . ."

It is clear that at an early age Sylvia Plath understood her writing to be a vocation and therefore inevitably a spiritual quest—although neither her background nor the culture of her youth provided her with the language or models of such spirituality. She saw writing as "a trust, a creative pledge to affirm life, hell and heaven, mud and marble." She was twenty years old when she wrote this pledge in her journal.

Greatness, perceived in others, can be held in mind as a radiant image. The icons come swiftly to mind: Mozart, Shakespeare, Rembrandt. They are examples of greatness. But the *ideal* of greatness exists differently. Its dynamism must be an act of faith. It is not a recognition, as perception of greatness in a particular artist or a scientist is. The ideal is an almost wholly imaginative act.

And the ideal inaugurates a struggle. As Plath says in a journal entry written in England about a month before she met Ted Hughes, "One cannot help but wish for those situations that make us heroic, living to the hilt of our total resources. Our cosmic fights, when I think the end of the world is come, are so many broken shells around our growth."

Although Plath considers briefly in her journal a "splurge of altruism" in which she might sacrifice herself "on the altar of the Cause with a capital C," there is no mention of what this Cause might be. She never identified deeply with any political cause for long.

She was casting her lot in the 1950s, and it seems clear, at least in the journals, that the struggle she knew she must engage in was interior. Not simply a struggle with her past—the impulse is not transparently autobiographical. Rather, the interiority is spiritual, an impulse toward transformation rather than confession. "I have long wanted to read and explore the theories of philosophy, psychology, national, religious and primitive consciousness," she says in the journal, linking her search to disciplines related to spiritual life.

In her *Chapters in a Mythology*, Judith Kroll sees in Plath's poetry "one overriding concern: the problem of rebirth or transcendence." The late poems in particular and Plath's definition of poetic vocation exhibit a calling which gave her "access to depths formerly reserved to primitive ecstatic priests, shamans and Holy men," as Kroll quotes Ted Hughes on the subject of Plath's sense of mission.

Plath herself seemed baffled by her fascination with "poetic identities of characters who commit suicide, adultery, or get murdered. . . ." She can only explain her attraction to these subjects by admitting in her journal that, for her, "What they say is True." This truth, though she does not embody it herself until the *Ariel* poems, is the truth of conflict, struggle—that which effects fundamental change. In these dramatic conflicts, Plath instinctively senses the theater of death and rebirth. The struggle is not simply a spectacle. It has a spiritual purpose, recognized as such:

> I want to get back to my more normal intermediate path where the *substance* of the world is permeated by my being: eating food, reading, writing, talking, shopping: so all is good in itself, and not just a hectic activity to cover up the fear that must face itself and duel itself to death, saying: A Life is Passing!

The real horror here (in strictly religious language, the real *sin*) is not death but the featureless "passing" of a life. Death is the greatest struggle, like those that leave "so many broken shells around our growth." It is not an end, but the deepest metaphor possible, literal and yet also a model for any re-creation of the self, any search for the real self beneath the litter of false selves of "hectic activity."

After her breakdown in 1953, Plath underwent a course of electric shock treatments which she always maintained had been administered incorrectly and almost electrocuted her. (One political event she notes in her work with eloquent feeling and particular horror is the death of the Rosenbergs.) She saw the experience as her own brutal high-tech death and resurrection. As she says in her journal of 1956, she wanted to write

> a detailed description of shock treatment, tight, blasting short descriptions with not one smudge of coy sentimentality. . . .

There will be no hurry, because I am too desperately venge-
ful now. But I will pile them up . . . the inevitable going
down the subterranean hall, waking to a new world, with no
name, being born again, and not of woman.

This is the selfless "will to bear witness" of the survivor, a
phenomenon Terrence Des Pres describes in *The Survivor,* his
book about writing from concentration camps. It is an urgency
shared by those who emerged from the death camps and felt
compelled to speak "for the others." It is not a self-involved mor-
bidity or a fascination with pain for its own sake. The *experience*
of such extremity is not the "witnessing." Only the writing of it,
only the telling, can approach transcendence.

The relation of a poet of mythic sensibility to autobiographical material is bound to be paradoxical. The unformed
autobiographical material is like a bright shred of plastic which
the poet breathes into, creating a balloon. The self is inflated and
floats aloft for all to see. Most American poets write such poems
of lyric autobiography.

A poet of mythic sensibility, however, seems compelled to
reach up and puncture this rounded autobiographical shape, to
end the severe limitation of meaning imposed by the merely personal use of autobiography. Plath, in the *Ariel* poems, is such a
mythic poet, grasping at the inflated balloon of her life, causing
it to collapse. This collapse of autobiography is a longing for a
more powerfully resonant voice, the voice of mythic significance.
Myth, after all, is that voice Plath identified in her journal, the
voice which allows the poet "to talk to everybody . . . as deeply
as possible."

Poets who undergo this collapse of the autobiographical self
in the service of an emerging mythic self speak in a rinsed, shining voice which moves from personal loss to spiritual gain.

Adrienne Rich, when her work began to reflect the experience of her feminist transformation, began to speak of the longing to be *useful*, to use rather than explore or exhibit the self:

> . . . I am an instrument in the shape
> of a woman trying to translate pulsations
> into images for the relief of the body
> and the reconstruction of the mind.

Judith Kroll notes a similar impulse in Plath's remark at the end of her life when she was writing the Ariel poems:

> I feel like a very efficient tool or weapon,
> used and in demand from moment to moment.

It is chilling, even repellent, to see the human recede into usefulness. It is deathly. But then, nothing less than death can cause the self to burn away, to cease to be the stuff of autobiography, lost in a new task, no longer personal, but a mythic tool—or as Plath feared—a weapon.

Why would anyone want to die? Even in a poem, why die? The pain of spiritual death keeps most poets—most people—safely within autobiography, repeating the lyric sensation of buoyancy that, after all, is what is usually meant by "being alive."

But once the autobiographical balloon bursts (usually through some form of unwilling loss), all the rules change. The laws of autobiography form the humanistic code of logic, of the beauty and supremacy of the body and the senses, and of lyric sensibility. In autobiography, I matter. In the post-autobiographical world, I am matter.

In this spiritual realm, where the narrative line of one's life has burned away, survival is based, as it is in art, on paradox: You must lose your soul to find it; die that you may live; surrender that you may be free. The world of spiritual life therefore is not unduly impressed by death. Or rather, it has found a central usefulness for death: Death is that which effects resurrection.

Still, pain is a fact, and the autobiographical self is firm about pain: It is bad. Or at least, it is too bad. The autobiographical self, after all, is no fool: It knows who must do the dying.

II

I can think of no contemporary poet who shares Plath's struggle as fully as does the philosopher Simone Weil. But to call Weil "a philosopher" in this century suggests a secular identity that misses her subject and her importance. She was, of course, a religious writer. She has much to say about suffering, that inevitable bridge from self to spirit. Weil's life is a fitting companion to Plath's attempt in her final poems to die and be born again, to locate her true, useful self under the false selves of ambition and personal loss, humiliation and impotence.

Simone Weil was, in her own fashion, a suicide. The starvation saint. She died in England in 1943, refusing nourishment and medical treatment for tuberculosis in an act of solidarity with those in the French Resistance. An unnecessary death, as far as the autobiographical self is concerned, a willful death, like any suicide. But for the moment, I read her—death and life—from the world where I think she finally lived, the post-autobiographical position of spiritual transformation, not from her "life," which was not her goal. It is the world also of Plath's great work, the *Ariel* poems.

More to the literary point, Plath and Weil share a voice—the scorched voice of the spiritual pilgrim. This is Weil: "Love is a sign of our wretchedness. God can only love himself. We can only love something else." And here is Plath:

I am too pure for you or anyone.
Your body
Hurts me as the world hurts God.

"We possess nothing in this world," Weil says, "other than the power to say I. This is what we should yield up to God, and that is what we should destroy." A statement made from the precarious bridge between autobiography and spirituality. To "carry one's cross," Weil explains, is precisely to cut down the tree of self, fashion it into the cross, "and then, carry it every day."

Weil calls this process "decreation." It is the way the self ceases to matter—and becomes matter. It is the experience Plath imagined during her *au pair* summer by the ocean in Swampscott: " . . . an awareness that . . . the fragile, miraculously knit organism which interprets . . , will move about for a little, then falter, fail, and decompose at last into the anonymous soil, voiceless, faceless, without identity."

Death is central to the usefulness the spirit seeks as its true identity. "We have to die in order to liberate a *tied-up* energy," Weil says, "in order to possess an energy which is free and capable of understanding the relationship of things." That may be the best definition of usefulness: an energy capable of understanding the relationship of things.

Once this truth is established, Simone Weil turns to pain, that constituent of death. In a central essay, "The Love of God and Affliction," she explores the essential role affliction plays in the "decreation" of self.

She is careful to distinguish affliction from "simple suffer-

ing." To her mind, "the great enigma of human life is not suffering but affliction." She makes several attempts in the essay to
characterize what she means by the word:

> Affliction is an uprooting of life, a more or less attenuated
> equivalent of death, made irresistably present to the soul by
> the attack or immediate apprehension of physical pain.

> Affliction is essentially a destruction of personality, a lapse
> into anonymity.

In the end, she presents a three-part definition of this form of
anguish, "which leaves the victim writhing on the ground like a
half-crushed worm":

> There is not real affliction unless the event which has
> gripped and uprooted a life attacks it directly or indirectly in
> all its parts, social, psychological, and physical. The social fac-
> tor is essential. There is not really affliction where there is not
> social degradation or the fear of it in some form or other.

Weil comes back several times in the essay to this triad which
forms affliction. "Extreme affliction," she writes, "means physical
pain, distress of soul and social degradation, all together. . . ." She
adds that "it is the essence of affliction that it is suffered unwill-
ingly." The dizzying sensation of senselessness, of uselessness,
must accompany its first stages. The "Why?" or "Why me?" of all
grievous laments. "There can be no answer to the 'Why?' of the
afflicted," Weil says, "because the world is necessity and not purpose."

   She pursues the point further. "People often reproach
Christianity," she says,

for a morbid preoccupation with suffering and grief. This is an error. Christianity is not concerned with suffering and grief, for they are sensations, psychological states, in which a perverse indulgence is always possible; its concern is with something quite different, which is affliction. Affliction is not a psychological state; it is a pulverization of the soul by the mechanical brutality of circumstances.

Weil goes on immediately to locate human purpose in the light of affliction: "It is our function in this world to consent to the existence of the universe." The autobiographical self dies hard— as it must to be true to itself. The cruellest aspect of affliction, as Weil describes it, is the guilty sensation of complicity it inspires in its victim. "Like a red-hot iron," affliction

> stamps the soul to its very depths with the contempt, the disgust, and even the self-hatred and sense of guilt and defilement which crime logically should produce but actually does not. Evil dwells in the heart of the criminal without being felt there. It is felt in the heart of the man who is afflicted and innocent.

This paradox may occur because affliction, with its trinity of suffering (physical, psychological, and social), allows no escape. It corrals the self within itself. This interiority invites the feeling of complicity. One feels attachment, even the attachment of a creator, to the affliction.

"Everything happens," Weil says, "as though the state of soul appropriate for criminals had been separated from crime and attached to affliction; and it even seems to be in proportion to the innocence of those who are afflicted." This sounds like Kafka—and it sounds like the lament of the educated twentieth-century person, the voice heard buzzing low from a therapist's office.

We accept as mythically apt Kafka's contortions, his elaborate guilt and infinitely patient descriptions of impotence and anguish. We see his devilish sensation of complicity in his own suffering as parts of his spiritual quest—and of ours. We understand his affliction, if we give over to him at all, as evidence of spiritual work of the highest sort. He is understood to be a religious writer. He said it himself: "Writing is prayer."

Why, then, have Sylvia Plath's contortions not seemed generative in this way? Partly, of course, because of the suicide, an act whose willfulness breaks the bond with affliction. Then too, the early writing about Plath claimed her work and life absolutely in what I've called a "sociological" way. The meaning of Plath's work necessarily remained political for quite some time because most of those writing about her claimed her as a model (or cautionary figure) of feminism.

There is another reason, though, for the unwillingness to read Plath for what she most certainly was trying to become: born again. The reason returns us to the original feminist reading of her work, the "sociological" reading. Our culture is not prepared to see its central myth played out by a female protagonist. Women have never been denied the right to suffer. But death-and-resurrection is a male role. As feminist theologians have been pointing out for two decades, in our world, God is a guy. Even if you don't believe in Him.

Affliction, following Simone Weil's three-part definition, sounds like the right word for Sylvia Plath's final months. She had recently given birth to her second child, had been hospitalized for an emergency appendectomy (the flowers in "Tulips" come from this hospitalization). She also was suffering from the worst winter London had experienced in decades. That covers physical pain. And certainly the psychological anguish of the breakup of her marriage (that tragically idealized marriage of two poets we read of in her journal) was accompanied by real or feared social humiliation. One need only read her poem "The Rival" to sense this anguish.

Social degradation is such an essential component of affliction because in a curious way it virtually ostracizes the victim while paradoxically casting her into a glaring public light. When the social degradation is caused by sexual humiliation, the pain is heightened. The victim feels terribly isolated, alone—*and* hideously exposed. "No day is safe from news of you," Plath says to her rival.

Unfortunately, Ted Hughes destroyed Plath's journals from this period—what would have been the *Ariel* journals—and so the personal voice of her affliction is not available to us for this crucial period as it is for her earlier years as a college student and young wife and mother.

Interestingly, martyrs (whose business it is to suffer) are not victims of affliction. "The martyrs who came into the arena singing as they faced the wild beasts," Simone Weil writes, "were not afflicted." Christ, however, like Job, "was afflicted. He did not die like a martyr. He died like a common criminal, in the same class as thieves, only a little more ridiculous. For affliction is ridiculous." Christ, in a sense, was a suicide: He could have saved himself. "Do you think that I cannot appeal to my Father," he says in the Garden of Gethsemane, rebuking one of his followers who strikes the slave of the high priest and cuts off his ear, "and he will at once send me more than twelve legions of angels? But how then should the scriptures be fulfilled, that it must be so?" Once again, the law of mythic life, not autobiographical life, is invoked: Obedience belongs to necessity, not to a willful search for purpose. And when he asks for the cup to be passed from him in the Garden and yet yields to "thy will," Jesus also accomplishes what Weil describes as "our function," our usefulness, on earth: to consent to the existence of all that is.

It is easy to confuse religion with piety—and in doing so, to miss a powerful spiritual current that displays no recognizable "holy" language. There is no piety in the real self, in the soul. Once the post-autobiographical voice is speaking, things have gone well beyond pietisms. There is only the urgency of utterance whose function, like the true human one, is "necessity." Plath did not define her search as religious as Simone Weil did. Plath put her faith not in religion, but in language, in the struggle to *say it*. But it is curious how often she mentions God and how persistently she uses religious imagery. Plath speaks with this voice in "Lady Lazarus":

> *Herr God, Herr Lucifer*
> *Beware*
> *Beware*

The inflation here feels very different from a lyric autobiographical inflation of the self and its experience. This heroic voice knows it is about to burst, to vaporize—to decreate itself. In "Tulips," Plath is quite explicit about the destruction of the autobiographical self:

> *I have let things slip, a thirty-year-old cargo boat*
> *Stubbornly hanging on to my name and address.*
> *They have swabbed me clear of my loving associations.*
> *Scared and bare on the green plastic-pillowed trolley*
> *I watched my tea set, my bureaus of linen, my books*
> *Sink out of sight, and the water went over my head.*
> *I am a nun now, I have never been so pure.*

The purity here is not the radiance of the "triumphant" self Robert Lowell heralded in his introduction to Ariel; it is not a Lawrentian "Look-we-have-come-through" feeling at all. It is death, all right, as the next stanza makes clear:

> *I didn't want any flowers, I only wanted*
> *To lie with my hands turned up and be utterly empty.*
> *How free it is, you have no idea how free—*
> *The peacefulness is so big it dazes you,*
> *And it asks nothing, a name tag, a few trinkets.*
> *It is what the dead close on, finally; I imagine them*
> *Shutting their mouths on it, like a Communion tablet.*

The Communion tablet of death—or death as Communion. You don't just burn away: You close on the Communion tablet, you become part of a Mystical Body. The point here is not the Christian imagery itself, but that Plath turned to it as the language that was available to her to describe the transformation she sought and intuited.

She was conscious of what she was trying to achieve. The *Ariel* we read is not the book she knew. The manuscript she put together began, as the published *Ariel* also does, with "Morning Song," a poem about the birth of her first child which begins with the word "Love." But the book as she organized it was to have ended with "Wintering" (now in the middle of the collection). The last word of this poem is "spring," and Plath wrote to her mother of her satisfaction in this clear framework for the book, that it ended with this most buoyant word.

After her death, however, Ted Hughes reordered the collection, making various changes. The second to last poem in the book now is "Edge," probably the last poem Plath wrote, a chillingly suicidal poem that begins with the famous lines

The woman is perfect.
Her dead

Body wears the smile of accomplishment,
The illusion of a Greek necessity

Flows in the scrolls in her toga,
Her bare

Feet seem to be saying:
We have come so far, it is over.

The final poem in the book is "Words," also one of her last poems, whose final lines are

From the bottom of the pool, fixed stars
Govern a life.

A very different ordering. In a sense, the Hughes organization is more accurate—autobiographically. Plath's ordering of the collection attests to her vision. In fact, according to Judith Kroll's careful piecing together of the writing of the final poems, none of the very last, frightening poems was in Plath's Ariel manuscript. She apparently wrote these grim poems (including "Totem," "Paralytic," "Mystic," "Words," "Contusion," and "Edge") after she put together the collection, after she left Devon where she and her husband had lived, and made her fateful way to London on her own with her two children.

Plath's intention would be more evident if her *Ariel* had been published, and the other, later poems had been collected separately. But perhaps this might have seemed an even worse travesty of the truth of things, a denial of the fact of her suicide.

Whichever ordering seems more apt or more respectful of

Plath's life and intentions, the fact remains that a woman who had written poems of genius, who had "decreated" the autobiographical self for the emergence of the "useful" mythic self, went off anyway and killed herself.

What went wrong? Is transformation a delusion? Or is literature just another lying cheat?

III

I wish to trust poetry. The desire persists that though it is made of nothing but words, poetry represents not only our lived life but our unlived life, the veiled existence of the soul. Simply: I believe poetry to be capable of religious revelation as religion itself is not.

Religion is typically too constrained by the systems and institutions that claim it; the progress of the soul is muffled as well by communal rites that draw the self into a group circle. The poet, however, travels solo, darting from sacred to profane and back and under and around . . . exactly as the pilgrim soul must in its fundamental vow to "consent to the existence of the universe."

Plath's suicide, like any suicide, can only be read as the deft play of a wild card. There is no *explaining* why a person chooses to end her life. Maybe the elusive power of chance, not our occasional sensations of joy, accounts for the tendency of non-suicides to find life engaging, in spite of everything. But even if I have no faith in the possibility of discovering "why" Plath committed suicide, those final poems may possess an indication of an imperfectly imagined transformation. In reading them again and again, I must acknowledge a lot of wishing on my part—the wish to trust poetry, the wish that spiritual transformation truly exists and can cleanse and reclaim a life whose "story," whose autobiography, has become a terrible hash.

Poetry's essence is not to show or to tell as we say of fiction, but to reveal. This means the poet is not really in control, great as that illusion may sometimes be, especially in highly formal poetry. The illusion is great in Sylvia Plath's poems. Her sense of form is meticulous, her imagination refined, severe, her vision at the extreme edge of the sayable.

Her early poems are weak exactly because her formal rigor is so absolute. Very little breath in those early poems, some collected in her first book, *The Colossus,* written by a young woman thumbing dutifully through her thesaurus. But in the *Ariel* poems, both the larger group Judith Kroll calls "mythic," and the final suicidal poems Ted Hughes added to the original manuscript, Plath's intentions are well served by her economy and control. She even says so explicitly in "Stings":

> *I am no drudge*
> *Though for years I have eaten dust*
> *And dried plates with my dense hair.*
>
> *And seen my strangeness evaporate,*
> *Blue dew from dangerous skin.*
> . . . .
>
> *It is almost over*
> *I am in control.*

The most startling thing about these poems of affliction that burn the autobiographical self into the mythic figure is not that they are filled with death. The problem seems to be that something is not sufficiently dead:

By the roots of my hair some god got hold of me.
I sizzled in his blue volts like a desert prophet.

—"THE HANGING MAN"

I see your voice
Black and leafy, as in my childhood,

A yew hedge of orders,
Gothic and barbarous, pure German.
Dead men cry from it.

—"LITTLE FUGUE"

I am only thirty.
And like the cat I have nine times to die.

—"LADY LAZARUS"

"Lady Lazarus," in fact, is about dying fruitlessly, again and again.
The references are to Plath's father's death (in this poem, in service to her mythic ordering, she places his death when she was
ten, though he really died when she was eight), then her own
suicide attempt at twenty, and the final preoccupation with death
at thirty.

But none of this dying gets the job done, it seems. There is
a terrible living on of the self, not just in memory, but in the
habit of the self to be wounded (afflicted) to no purpose. "I suffer," Plath says in her journal, "but I do not become
Shakespeare." Or the purpose is the cruel amusement of the
crowd (Weil's social degradation):

The peanut-crunching crowd
Shoves in to see

Them unwrap me hand and foot—
the big strip tease.

—"LADY LAZARUS"

What she feels capable of is cheap disclosure, a strip tease; what she requires is the miracle, resurrection.

Plath was "done for," as she puts it in "Death & Co.," perhaps because she was unable to conceive of transformation as a gesture, as a movement of the self, achieved as a gift received rather than as an accomplishment performed. In "Daddy," the poem about her first death, she is patricidal by the second stanza, in part because the father is perceived as a piece of statuary:

Daddy, I have had to kill you,
You died before I had time—
Marble-heavy, a bag full of God,
Ghastly statue with one grey toe.

The gruesome mechanism that passes for living in "The Applicant" is another evidence of this grimly static perception of the self:

A living doll, everywhere you look.
It can sew, it can cook,
It can talk, talk, talk.

The next stanza insists, positively sells, the self as if it were an object:

It works, there is nothing wrong with it.
You have a hole, it's a poultice.
You have an eye, it's an image.

These images of the old self are supposed to die, in order to effect transformation. It's their not dying that causes the problem. They don't die because Plath keeps retrieving them as pure, controlled images, heavily refined. She frames everything—which stops it, true enough, but hardly kills it. In fact, she memorializes what should go dead into the sepulchre and disappear for good.

It is worth remembering that the first evidence of Christ's resurrection in the Gospels is not the discovery of his body, but the absence of his body from the tomb: no icon. In Matthew, Mary Magdalene and "the other Mary" go to the sepulchre. An angel appears and says, "Do not be afraid; for I know you seek Jesus who was crucified. He is not here; for he is risen, as he said. Come, see the place where he lay."

The women, we are told in Mark and Luke, have come with spices for the body. But there is no body. The first evidence is not of the transfigured, risen body, but of the absence of the bodily self. (In John there is mention of the linen burial clothes used to wrap the body; seeing these bandages, John, "the one whom Jesus loved, . . . believed.") And Thomas the Doubter, who needs not only to see but to touch the body, goes down in history as someone who missed the whole point of the resurrection.

It may well be that literature cannot do what Plath went to it for. Her "problem," or her question, was religious, yet she remained rigorously literary in her strategies and resources.

She seems aware, sometimes desperately so, of the narrow imagistic prison she has written herself into. One of the last poems is aptly titled "Paralytic." In "Years," she cries out for action as only the impotent can:

> *What I love is*
> *The piston in motion—*
> *My soul dies before it.*

Once again transformation has been imaged (as the piston, an object), not imagined as movement. There is a pathetic wistfulness here. "I simply cannot see where there is to get to," she says pitifully in that beautiful poem, "The Moon and the Yew Tree."

This frustration over movement and destination is significant. After all, as Ted Hughes arranged *Ariel*, the last words in the book are "fixed stars/Govern a life." Any sign of movement seems threatening:

> *How far is it?*
> *How far is it now? The gigantic gorilla interior*
> *Of the wheels move, they appall me.*
>   —"GETTING THERE"

This poem, which seems to derive from a dream, is replete with images of broken or bloody or burned figures, "a hospital of dolls," "legs, arms piled." The repeated insistent question—"How far is it?"—covers the more burning question of where she is going. To death, of course; she is clear in the final lines when she speaks of stepping from "the black car of Lethe." But she has already admitted, "I cannot undo myself, and the train is steaming." The train, the conveyance, not the willing self, is what has gone on this journey. The self is dragged, not carried, along, "and I in agony."

There is a great deal of exhaustion in the *Ariel* poems:

> *And it exhausts me to watch you*
> *Flickering like that, wrinkly and clear red, like*
> *the skin of a mouth.*
>   —"POPPIES IN JULY"

> *I am nobody; I have nothing to do with explosions.*
>   —"TULIPS"

I am exhausted, I am exhausted—
Pillars of white in a blackout of knives.

—"Bee Meeting"

Effort and impotence and exhaustion—the heavy burden of one who feels personal effort is meant to solve things. Much earlier, as an achingly ambitious college girl, Plath tried to write her way out of a serious depression, "gathering forces into a tight ball for the artistic leap."

She admits in the journal entry that it is all "dreams, private dreams. But if I work? And always work to think, and know and practice technique always?" If she practices always to be perfect, especially practices technique, that controllable method of transformation, then shouldn't everything come out right?

The old metaphor—that life is a journey—inevitably becomes the figure used to express spiritual transformation. This metaphor is so embedded in our understanding of spiritual life that it is hardly perceived as a metaphor. Journey, quest, pilgrimage—we use these words as a matter of course, unconsciously.

Yet Sylvia Plath, who was so clearly engaged in the work of spiritual transformation, stumbled over this metaphor, unable to use it, unable to give herself the favor of understanding she was on a trip, that the unexpected would come her way, and that this was not her responsibility but her gift.

Because she could not see herself on a journey, except the forced passage of a refugee crammed into a cattle car, she also could not imagine a destination. "There is no terminus," she says in "Totem" (a very late poem), "only suitcases." No journey, just baggage.

When there *is* movement (as in "Getting There"), it is usually grimly mechanized. "The engine is killing the track," she writes in the first line of this poem. The journey (the track) itself is destroyed by the pilgrim—if an engine can even be called a pilgrim. "I cannot run," she says in "Bee Meeting," "I could not run without having to run forever." Once again, no destination, just eternal effort.

In place of a journey with a destination, Plath poses exhausted striving and the framed images of memory (the snapshots of autobiography), the horrified stills of the old life:

> *My husband and child smiling out of the family photo;*
> *Their smiles catch onto my skin, little smiling hooks.*
>
> —"TULIPS"

It may be that the central metaphor of the journey is potentially more troubling, even threatening, to a woman than to a man. After all, if it is the central metaphor of our culture, the quest is a male metaphor, primitively related to the hunt. The ancient myth for women, on the other hand, is tied to the icon (the virgin, the mother) and to a rooted place (the home, the hearth).

But to have a history which, being a *story* (an autobiography), is wounded by plot and its fluency of action, the poet cannot remain an icon, a statue, a fixed body. The poet must take the trip—not just take the pictures. Plath hangs on to the attempt to frame the self in a picture, even as she is ripping herself up in a frustrated attempt at spiritual change.

Death and resurrection. She knows someone must die. But what is resurrection? A complete trust in death? Or is it faith? And what is this "new self?" A baby? There are a lot of babies in Plath's poems, "awful babies," weird and creepy figures. Terrible

babies, most terrible when they are presented as statuary. Even in
the first *Ariel* poem, "Morning Song," one of the more radiant
poems in the collection, the newborn child is immediately seen
as a "new statue./ In a drafty museum. . . ." There are many of
these frozen baby statues in the poems, one of the most chilling
groupings in "Death & Co.":

> *He tells me how sweet*
> *The babies look in their hospital*
> *Icebox, a simple*
>
> *Frill at the neck,*
> *Then the flutings of their Ionian*
> *Death-gowns.*

Without the saving metaphor of the journey, which does
not explain anguish but rather gives it location and renders it
potentially useful as metaphor, the road of the pilgrim soul is
an exhausting conveyor belt, leading nowhere but back to a
repetition of wished-for embarkations. Even that stylistic habit
of Plath's, the triple beat of the verb or of central nouns,
seems, in this light, not so much an insistence as an impotent
stutter:

> *It can talk, talk, talk.*
> . . . .
> *Will you marry it, marry it, marry it.*
>
> —"THE APPLICANT"

> . . . *These are the isolate, slow faults*
> *That kill, that kill, that kill.*
>
> —"ELM"

Now I am milkweed silk, the bees will not notice.
They will not smell my fear, my fear, my fear.

—"The Bee Meeting"

If Sylvia Plath has a muse it is the moon. In "The Moon and the Yew Tree" she even says, "The moon is my mother." But this moon-mother "is not sweet like Mary." Like anything Plath is almost willing to trust, there is an edge, an aloof harshness to the image.

"How I would like to believe in tenderness," she says later in the poem. Probably her most honest, most exhausted line. Unlike the trust expressed in her early journal for "characters who commit suicide, adultery, or get murdered" because "what they say is True," evidence of kindness is a signal of weakness.

Plath, who has taken on impossible interior burdens, doesn't believe in kindness, but in accomplishment: "Why am I obsessed with the idea I can justify myself by getting manuscripts published?" Plath's ambition, by which she seeks to save or find herself ("But if I work? And always work to think, and know and practice technique always?"), is the outer sign of a relentless willfulness that fills her being.

When spiritual writers speak of the "death of the self," they mean the death of the will. If Sylvia Plath was loyal to her will, that instrument of control, it is also hard to think of a writer who was more faithful to her terror, the radical emotion of vulnerability, than she was. Plath retained a remarkable loyalty to her desperation. In no single book of poetry in the past quarter century has private concision voiced as eloquently as *Ariel* does, the interior urge for transformation.

And for women certainly there will always be the grave

sense of history having been made in the *Ariel* poems: Here, finally, the ancient struggle is described in female terms, the beast of living wrestled down to the mat by a woman, fiercely employing her—our—images in terrible, contorted holds until the effort failed, and the light went elsewhere.

March 21, California, the Santa Cruz mountains washing into each other in hillocky mounts and slides, the spring green dotted black here and there by grazing cattle. Above, the pure arc of the sky, the fog of the last several days finally burned away. Off in the far distance, making the end of the world a silver glint, the Pacific is pooled. The light out there is latched by the horizon's delicate hinge linking sky and sea.

No eye is as credulous of landscape as a Midwesterner's: The habit of flatness and soft surfaces creates a childish eagerness to believe all this improbable mountain-sea-sky melodrama. The dirty rusks of the neighborhood snowbanks back home in Saint Paul are there behind me somewhere, but I've been here a week now, and carry a wildflower book on walks, diligently labeling the facts of spring: Scotch broom, trillium, meadow-foam . . .

I cannot imagine killing myself. Like everyone, I've sometimes wished I were dead, but have never inflicted a wound: a habit of being interested in the next thing saves us non-suicides, I suppose, at dangerous moments. Last week, the filthy snowbanks of Saint Paul, this week the sea: Good things sometimes turn up. That is enough for some of us. I found myself saying, as I took a hike in this glory of a landscape yesterday, "Great God, great God." Not simply an exclamation. It was a prayer, and rose of its own volition. Maybe the only real prayers *are* exclamations, brief, unbidden, hardly belonging to the speaker.

Then at night, almost finished with this, typing at the furious pace I learned years ago when I worked as a temp for Kelly Girl, I was halted abruptly by a power failure. The computer stopped like a stone. The study lamp went dark, returned with a brief wheeze of sepia light, and then closed down entirely. Everything went black, and stayed black.

This morning we found out what had happened. A man, crazy and jealous, shot his girlfriend from his car while she was driving along one of these narrow mountain roads in her car. She crashed into a power pole—dead. Then the man went streaking off in his car, sheered off a ridge—dead too, probably a suicide though it's hard to say for sure.

The bizarre sensation of connection, person to person: tapping away here at top speed, my current cut off by a woman's death, the knowledge now that my inconvenience was her end. That casual link, the faint flicker of odd light from the study lamp before everything went pure black. The weight of chance in a life, the relative destinies we bear and occasionally touch across the great, vibrating vacancy.

Now the power is back, and out the window the colossal miracle of this landscape slants to the endless sea.

I said I wished to trust poetry. I wished also, like many women of my generation, to trust ambition, the power of personal accomplishment, rather than the old roles of dependence and service. And, reading Plath again, I have even wished for her sake that it might have been so—that she could have felt justified by getting manuscripts published, by working hard and practicing technique always.

But it's way past time to quit wishing. Or to mistake wishing with prayer. "Writing is prayer," Kafka, that most afflicted one, said. And writing, certainly, isn't wishing; it is witnessing. But to what do you testify? To your own desperation? Plath did that. To your desires? But isn't that back to wishes again?

There is a way, and Sylvia Plath knew it as a girl writing out of the genius of her loneliness at Swampscott, facing the other ocean, locating herself by its immensity:

> A consuming love . . . of the clean unbroken sense that the rocks which are nameless, the waves which are nameless, the ragged grass which is nameless, are all defined momentarily through the consciousness of the being who observes them.

This is the transforming self, the useful being who "with the sun burning into rock, and flesh, and wind ruffling grass and hair" experiences "an awareness that the blind immense unconscious impersonal and neutral forces will endure." She recognizes herself as "the fragile, miraculously knit organism which interprets" all of this and "endows [it] with meaning." That miraculously knit organism which interprets was, in Sylvia Plath's case, too relentless to safeguard that very fragility.

But on the washed rocks of Swampscott, she expressed with serenity her function which was to "move about for a little, then falter, fail, and decompose at last into the anonymous soil, voiceless, faceless, without identity." A statement that is sister to Simone Weil's understanding that "it is our function in this world to consent to the existence of the universe."

Whether the peace of that acquiescence, that anonymity, was Sylvia Plath's on this earth is unknown to us. Still, she imagined it once, which is to say she lived it once. That counts.

And if wishes refuse to be denied voice, it should be possible to advance a small wish on her behalf, something merely ceremonial, but in the spirit of valediction: That something might end with what she intended as her final word in the book she understood was her claim to genius, the book which would place her among the poets after her death.

For in the distance, the sun is cutting the Pacific clean silver, and it is the first day of spring.

The Invention of
Autobiography:
Augustine's *Confessions*

*I*n the year 397, a Catholic bishop named Aurelius Augustinus, living in the provincial Mediterranean seaport of Hippo Regius (now Annaba, Algeria), managed to compose, over the course of a year filled with exhausting pastoral duties, a strange work he gave the title "my confessions in thirteen books." This is the intensely personal document we now think of as the West's first autobiography.

Augustine was forty-three at the time of its composition, a baptized Catholic for ten years, a bishop for two. He was in bad shape—sick with a recurring inflammation, and disheartened by schismatic attacks on his ecclesiastic authority and politically motivated rumors about his sensational past. Against his own desire to lead a contemplative life, he had served as pastor to the Catholics of Hippo since 391 when he had been pressed into service as their priest. He wept through the whole ordination ceremony.

No wonder. His ordination pulled him back into the world's fray. As an exultant convert in 387, Augustine imagined a genteel life of intellectual pursuits surrounded by like-minded friends in a kind of laid-back monastic setting, first in the glorious region near Lake Como, later in his North African homeland. Instead, he had been forced into the duties of the priesthood by a fractious congregation, and finally was called on to serve as its bishop in 395.

With his baptism Augustine had turned his back on the fast-track career and public ambitions that had driven him as a young man who was, as he says in Book VI, "all hot for honors, money, marriage." The leisurely life he had in mind after his baptism was an honorable one in the Roman world where the notion of a job was degraded to drudgery by its association with slavery. A life of gracious ease—the Latin *otium cum dignitate*—was the classical ideal for the truly civilized man. Such a man would probably never be rich or powerful, but he had chosen "the better part," as Jesus says in the Gospel of those who reflect and ponder. This choice conferred a certain status money could not buy. What is more, the man of cultivated idleness had all the time in the world for study, writing and art—and for religion. The soul, as both pagan and Christian ancients knew, loves leisure.

In Augustine's Roman North Africa a bishop was no such gentleman of leisure. He was an ecclesiastical and liturgical figure, but also a kind of magistrate, assaulted by his congregation with small-claims disputes, and forced to beseech a haughty civil service on their behalf. Until well after midday Augustine might listen to the feuds and disgruntlements of his flock. He could waste the better part of his day hanging around the corridors of power, waiting to plead a case with a disdainful bureaucrat. It was public advocacy work, demanding, fitful, always presenting itself as urgent, but opposed to the intellectual and spiritual life he craved.

Augustine was a writer, after all, a rhetorician by training. The frets and feuds of other people and the endless middle management of his bishopric nibbled his day away. He complained, as writers always do, of not having time to write, or even to read. In a letter to a friend he described himself as "a man who writes as he progresses and who progresses as he writes." Not to write was not to think, really not to live.

Against this backdrop of the inexorable and, no doubt to him alarmingly public, spiral of his life, Augustine stops in his tracks (or pauses—perhaps the more accurate word) to write his urgent inquiry to his God. The *Confessions* are, among other things, the desperate gesture of a writer blocked from his work, seeking again the intimate embrace and healing intelligence of language.

In Milan on the solemn Easter Sunday night of April 24–25, 387, according to the ritual all Catholic catechumens underwent, Augustine had stepped alone, stark naked, into the pool of the basilica's baptistry, and emerged from the waters to be clothed in a white robe, knowing himself utterly changed. This moment after his slow conversion to Catholicism following years of frantic religious searching remained an unequivocal treasure to him for the rest of his long life. Yet the *Confessions* are not a testament of triumphal conversion. They are a solemn act of renewal. We can recognize in Augustine's book the later impulse of Dante's midlife declaration when "in the middle of the journey of our life," as he says in the famous first lines of the *Divine*

Comedy, "I came to myself within a dark wood where the straight way was lost." ← The quest begins

This location—the adult midpoint of uncertainty and even anguish—is the site of autobiography. Augustine does not write his life as an act of reminiscence. Nor is memory his tool for a magisterial summing up. Memory is, first, a captivating mystery. It is a faculty of mind so grand that Augustine turns to the heroic images of architecture to describe it: "the vast mansions of memory," "the immense court of my memory." But even mansions and palaces, those classical models for the storehouse of recollection, are not extensive enough to suggest his memory: "for there sky and earth and sea are readily available. . . ."

In Book X, Augustine's majestic meditation on memory, he sees his own memory as an "exceedingly great, a vast, infinite recess" or as another translation has it, "a spreading limitless room within me." Memory is the only sure road to self-knowledge, and therefore provides access to the Divine which is Augustine's real destination. This is so because "in the immense court of my memory . . . I come to meet myself." Given such towering belief in the powers of memory, writing autobiography begins to look inevitable, even necessary. For autobiography is memory's articulation. The *confessio* is the voice of memory, murmuring from its mysterious cavern.

There had been autobiographies, Christian and pagan, before Augustine's. The Catholic Church, since 310 the orthodox religion of the Roman Empire, was less than a century away from outlaw status. The harrowing, sangfroid testimonials written at the edge of martyrdom by the early saints were a traditional genre for pious Christians. Lacking the drama of these martyrs, refined late-Roman Christians could still be edified by the inner struggles of good-and-evil in the formula conversion tales of their contemporaries. The fact that Christianity, unlike

[handwritten margin note, right side:] is memory is unfaithful, factoring, varying across time + circumstance

[handwritten margin note, right side:] I disagree: I say forgetting leads to self-knowledge; letting go of the past and being in the present is the only way to the divine.

[handwritten note, bottom:] Critique of class — need to incl. non-western writings in this section; perhaps Confucian or Lao-Tzu

either Judaism or the religions of the Greeks and Romans, was a cult founded on the narrative of a single life—Jesus of Nazareth—may help to explain the appeal of life stories in Christian literary culture—and continuing into our own. Even further back, the pagan West had honored the notion of the self as the pathway of spiritual ascent. "Know yourself," the doorway to the oracle at Delphi counseled. Knowing yourself had always been, for the West, just a short step away from writing yourself.

Still, Augustine's autobiography struck even his contemporaries as new, startling even. It shocked them for reasons different from the way we might be shocked, perhaps, but it is still possible to feel their amazement. (Part of *our* shock is simply that someone writing sixteen centuries ago can seem so much like us.) Here was a book, most likely written by hand in private, but intended to be read aloud by small groups of educated Christians (and open-minded erudite pagans), a book handed around in a kind of *samizdat* circulation. It was greeted by the intense, if rarefied, buzz we might recognize from a coffeehouse poetry reading where aficionados know an original voice when they hear one.

Some of his first readers had theological and even stylistic criticisms of Augustine's shattering book: It was too mystical, it was too flashy. But certainly one of the things that made Augustine's readers gasp was not his admission of lust, but his acknowledgment that, after conversion, indeed even as a bishop of the Church, he is still searching and speculating about his God and himself. "These writings are no true confessions of mine," he admits to God (and to his readers) about his grasp of scripture, "unless I confess to you, 'I do not know.' " Augustine is not the mysteriously serene convert, but an anxious soul, more inflamed than ever.

So, I must ask: Is there no writing for writing's
sake? I guess even chinese _art_ of writing, callig.,
is a meditation — not contemplation though.

It is the act of being in the moment. In that sense
it is art for art's sake.

It's similar to Tibetan sand paintings, created
through hours/days of hard work, which is
then destroyed to remind us of the
impermanence of all things.

Theology aside, what may separate us most from
Augustine is the way we read. A modern emblem of lonely indi-
viduality is the image of the urban commuter, head bent to
open book, reading silently on a jammed subway. Our assumption that reading is an inner, essentially solitudinous activity
would strike an ancient as eccentric. There was no publishing as
we know it, of course, in Augustine's world. Communal reading
or recitation of books was so much a given of literate life that it
went unremarked. When, however, Augustine first glimpses his
mentor Ambrose, bishop of Milan, reading alone, silently to
himself, he describes the act in Book VI of the *Confessions* like
a fascinated anthropologist writing a field note on an exotic
tribal custom: ". . . his eyes would travel across the pages and his
mind would explore the sense, but his voice and tongue were
silent."

This observed moment was not simply an oddity for
Augustine; it unlocked for him a new way of imagining a relationship with the Word. The *Confessions* are startling—to his
ancient audience as well as to us—largely because Augustine has
found a way to reveal the privacy of a mind thinking. This is the
narrative engine that drives autobiography: consciousness, not
experience, is the galvanizing core of a personal story.

Augustine does not present us with the result of thought in
a bundled package; he confronts us with the passionate nature of
the pursuit of meaning as it courses through a life. He reveals the
urgency of the soul's quest. Thinking and feeling merge in a way
quite shocking—and thrilling. Augustine observed Ambrose
deep in the meditation of scripture, and now in the *Confessions*
we observe Augustine in profound contemplation of his life. He

But, how can we separate
experience from consciousness?
And vice-versa? Indeed
we should not.

saw the nakedness of Ambrose's mental search when he caught him reading silently in the Milan cathedral. Now, in the book of his life, Augustine makes of himself that searching figure, alone but companioned by his own questing mind, objectified by the act of writing. "I have become an enigma to myself," he says, "and herein lies my sickness." Saying this, he becomes the West's first existential hero, both protagonist and narrator of his own inner struggle.

Literate ancients lived somewhere between a communal oral tradition and our own book culture. Books are objects to us, things we buy, borrow, carry around. But for men like Augustine, books, while they were formally composed texts rather than oral folklore, were not wholly material. To own a book in Augustine's time might mean to memorize it, not to possess a copy of it. The ancients were monsters of memorization, committing whole treatises and much of scripture to memory in ways unfathomable to us. They performed this discipline for the most practical reason: The mind was the surest, cheapest way to maintain a library.

"To read" meant to listen. Public recitation made reading a kind of team sport. The audience might interrupt the reader to pose questions, to make comments, to pursue the subject of the document, spinning away and back again to the text itself. When Augustine considers the conundrum of Ambrose's silent reading, for example, he finally puzzles out a likely reason for it: The old bishop "might be apprehensive that if he read aloud, and any closely attentive listener were doubtful on any point, or the author he was reading used any obscure expressions, he would have to stop and explain various difficult problems. . . ."

The culture of memorization affected composition as well. The treasury of memorized texts packed in the writer's mind made "writing," like "reading," more densely communal than we

[marginal handwritten note, left margin, vertical:] NOT JUST to ENTERTAIN.

[handwritten note, bottom of page:] This gets back to the act of writing as public — never private. The moment you write anything you do so with the knowledge, however unconscious, that someone may someday read those writings.

can easily understand. A text was a buzz and murmur of voices, literary chamber music, not solo performance. The call and reply between a writer's own voice and his memorized texts created a rich, polyphonic texture, an antiphony of language where leitmotifs of prized quotations suddenly wink and gleam from new prose settings.

Augustine doesn't just quote the Psalms in the *Confessions*; they penetrate his text like a theme he can improvise endlessly, proving their protean nature and his own virtuoso intimacy with them. He truly has the Psalms "by heart." He tunes his lyre to David's, and makes his own music from monotheism's primal songs and laments.

*T*he first nine books of the *Confessions* feel familiar to us. They are what we think of as autobiography. Augustine casts before us incident and vignette, sketch and portrait, stringing these bright gemstones on the story line of his life as he writes his way from his birth in 354 in Thagaste (now Souk Ahras in the hills of eastern Algeria) to the bittersweet period following his baptism when his mother dies at the Roman port of Ostia as she and Augustine and their circle wait to sail home to Africa.

In these nine chapters of his life, Augustine muses about his babyhood, and even beyond that to his time in the womb, searching what a psychologized modern would call "the unconscious" for hints and clues to his nature. He is clearly troubled by the mystery of existence: "I do not know where I came from," he says with surprisingly agnostic wonder.

Augustine begins his great portrait of his devout Berber Christian mother in Book I as he reminds the Lord how he nursed at her breast, taking in, he knows, much more than milk.

Monica's personality storms and rainbows over the entire book. She is her son's biggest fan and greatest nag. She is also "my mother, my incomparable mother!" Her concern about her son verges on obsession. "Like all mothers, though far more than most," Augustine the bishop writes, still confounded after all these years by her passionate attachment, "she loved to have me with her." She follows him to the dock when he is about to leave Africa for Rome, weeping and wailing, begging him either to stay or to take her with him. Finally desperate to be rid of her, he lies about the time of his departure and makes his escape.

A good try, but Monica, of course, gets her way, on earth and in heaven. She follows Augustine to Rome and then to Milan when he secures a plum teaching position there. She prays him into the Church with more than pious wishes: She has a mother's spooky clairvoyance, and assures him she *knows* he will find his way to baptism. Her prophecy climaxes in Book IX during their mutual mystical experience in Ostia.

In marked contrast to his rhapsodic writing about Monica, Augustine mentions his father with telling coolness. Patricius was a small-time farmer who remained a pagan until receiving baptism on his deathbed. He was neither a success in life nor a questing soul. He died when Augustine was eighteen and he cast only a faint shadow on his son's consciousness. Augustine was his mother's son, and knew it.

No incident is too small for Augustine in the *Confessions*—provided it has metaphoric value. He is a gifted writer, after all, a pro, and he knows very well that his description of his boyhood theft of pears from a garden—a purely willful act because he didn't even want to eat the pears—rings a change on the first theft in another Garden.

He reports his first prayer—"not to be beaten at school." And reminds God that in response to this first intercession "You did not hear my prayer. . . ." Augustine recalls the harshness of his school days and the cruelty of his teachers with the scorekeeping precision of a true memoirist, immune to the irritating wisdom of forgiving and forgetting. The slap of his boyhood humiliations and the still-tender skin of the adult bishop who recounts them ring down the centuries. "We loved to play," he explains heatedly, appealing to God as if to a referee in a ghostly game of yore, "and we were punished by adults who nonetheless did the same themselves. But whereas the frivolous pursuits of grown-up people are called 'business,' children are punished. . . . Moreover, was the master who flogged me any better himself? If he had been worsted by a fellow-scholar in some pedantic dispute, would he not have been racked by even more bitter jealousy than I was when my opponent in a game of ball got the better of me?" Still arguing his case after all these years.

We see him grow into a young intellectual, sharpening his knives of argument, engaged in his first philosophical battles. The Manichees, a gnostic sect whose dualism greatly appeals to him at first, later become a grave disappointment. He hopscotches from Manicheism to a fashionable skepticism, then into a mystical Neoplatonism that leads him finally to the threshold of the Church. He enumerates his hesitations about Catholicism, and presents the process, both intellectual and spiritual, that leads him finally to the Baptistry in Milan. We feel the circumspection of his mind: After listening carefully to the great bishop Ambrose he says coolly, "I realized that the Catholic faith . . . was in fact intellectually respectable." This is not the response of a credulous seeker, but the balanced judgment of an educated, upwardly mobile provincial intent on climbing in Roman society, a classical Latin scholar still slightly uneasy with the folk elements in biblical texts. The urgency of his search for truth never leaves his story. It is the ground beat of the tale.

why not?
People often read
Darwin's Bio.

But we would not read the *Confessions* down the centuries if they were the testimony of an intellectual's struggles, no matter how passionately told. It is passion itself that makes Augustine alive to us. He insists that we understand this about him: Well after his intellectual questions had been answered, he continues to resist conversion because, to him, baptism means chastity. In fact, the most famous line in the *Confessions* is the prayer of his hot adolescence: "Grant me chastity and self-control, but please not yet."

Augustine was not the promiscuous lover of popular imagination—or of his own description. From the age of nineteen he lived in complete and apparently happy fidelity with his girlfriend, a woman of lower rank with whom marriage was not a possibility. We never learn her name. She and Augustine have a child together, a son named Adeodatus (Gift of God) who, like Monica and several youthful friends, compose his intimate circle.

When Augustine does abandon this lover of his youth, it is to make a prudent marriage, a logical career move which Monica promoted. The break is shattering. His girlfriend, he says, "was ripped from my side. . . . So deeply was she engrafted into my heart that it was left torn and wounded and trailing blood." While he waited two years for the girl to whom he was engaged to reach marriageable age, he says, with the crudeness of a broken heart, that he "got myself another woman." But even this indulgence does not help: "The wound inflicted on me by the earlier separation did not heal. . . . After the fever and the immediate acute pain had dulled, it putrefied, and the pain became a cold despair."

*I*s it possible to read the *Confessions* today with the same urgency that Augustine brought to writing them? This is not simply a modern's self-admiring question about a late fourth-century book's "relevance" to our own secular age. It is a question Augustine would have appreciated, believing as he did in sorting things out for oneself. He refused, for example, to accept the glossy reputation of Faustus, the Manichee sage who proved, when frankly questioned, to be a charming phony. The blunt question of Augustine's appeal to the modern reader must be posed.

The answer lies in Augustine's literary self. With all the theological and cultural differences and all the history that divide us from Augustine's first readers, our recognition of the originality and power of the *Confessions* resides fundamentally in the same place—in his voice. Not because his is a magically "modern" voice from antiquity, somehow chumming up to the reader. In any case, the book isn't written to us.

It is addressed expressly to God. *Magnus es, Domine*, it begins: Great are you, Lord. Augustine claims in the first breath of the *Confessions* that his intention is the innate one—"we humans," he says simply, ". . . long to praise you." But the real voice of the book is one of inquiry. He wants to *know*. At times it is heartbreaking, even comic, to see Augustine struggle with the mystery of existence. "Was there nothing before . . . except the life I lived in my mother's womb?" he asks in Book I. "But then, my God, my sweetness, what came before that? Was I somewhere else? Was I even someone? I have nobody to tell me. . . . Are you laughing at me for asking you these questions?" Augustine is willing to look foolish, even before God, if it will get him below the surface of things. This willingness to risk being a fool for the truth, which is all that literary courage is, keeps Augustine young for the ages.

The habitual way of approaching the *Confessions* is to see Augustine as a penitent, a man gazing with horror at his sinful

[handwritten marginalia: How does searching for some truth alter how we write. As opposed to accepting that we can never know the Truth]

past from the triumphant refuge of his conversion. Maybe the *Confessions* would have been such a book if Augustine had written them in 387, the year of his baptism and the death of Monica. It was certainly the great high-low year of his existence, the pivot of his life. But it is fully ten years after his baptism (a harrowing adult initiation experience, a true cult act signaling a changed life, not to be confused with the mild christening ceremonies of our own times) when Augustine turns to write the great searching book of his life.

The adjective is significant: What, after all, is a converted Christian properly searching for? Isn't the definition, the whole meaning of religious conversion, precisely that the great answer has been found, that one has moved from uncertainty to conviction? In its ardent, insistent questioning, the *Confessions* is not an ode. Like the Psalms of David, Augustine's great rhapsodic-furious model, it is a call to attention. But then, perhaps to call out to God, to demand a response, *is* to praise, though not in the pietistic way we routinely mistake as religious. The core of praise, for Augustine, lies in the fact that he, like all human beings, is so thoroughly God's creature that his *confessio*, his life quest for God, can never be finished. He was created to be that creature who beats its fists against the breast of the divine. "For Thou has made us for Thyself," Augustine says on the first page of the *Confessions*, "and our hearts are restless till they rest in Thee."

Augustine's longing to know is not merely intellectual. He must know as one knows through love—by being known. *Deus, noverim te, noverim me,* he prays. God, let me know You and know myself. Probably no one since Job has inquired of his God as desperately and commandingly. Like Job, Augustine sees prayer as a form of thinking, a way of seeking truth, not a pious form of wishing. But Job is a character in a great primeval tale. Augustine, in the fine paradox of autobiography, is a character in a story *and* the narrator of that character. He bears in his voice the blood-beat of time. He belongs not to myth, but to history. As we do.

*B*ut why the final four books? Why ruin the narrative symmetry of his life story by attaching a long speculative essay on memory (Book X), chapters on time and eternity, and a final intense reading of the opening lines of the Book of Genesis (Books XI, XII, and XIII)? Perhaps the speculation on memory makes sense in an autobiography which is rooted in personal recollection. But after writing the sublime scene in Ostia with Monica, and recounting her final hours and his grief in Book IX, Augustine moves smoothly, without explanation or apology, as if it were the most natural thing in the world, through the long chapter on memory into an extended allegorical meditation on the opening lines of the Creation story of Genesis as if this too were "his life."

In fact, the movement from his life to his reading of Genesis is not smooth—it is ablaze. The writing becomes more, not less, urgent. *His* story, for Augustine, is apparently only part of the story. There is a certain logic at work. Having constructed himself in the first nine books, Augustine rushes on to investigate how God created the universe—how God, that is, created him. And all of us, all of *this*. Reading Genesis with his laser-beam gaze is a form of concentrated life. Reading, pondering, *is* experience. For Augustine *lectio* is not "reading" as we might think of it. For him, as for his teacher Ambrose, it is an acute form of listening. It is an act filled with the pathos of the West: The individual, alone in a room, puts finger to page, and follows the Word, attempting to touch the elusive Lord, the mystical *That*

Which Is, last seen scurrying down the rabbit hole of Creation: *In the beginning God created.* . . .

The voice of God is speaking on that page. Augustine, grappling with Genesis in his study, is no less heated—more so really—than Augustine struggling famously with "the flesh." He invents autobiography not to reveal his memory of his life but to plumb the memory of God's creative urge.

"My mind burns to solve this complicated enigma," he says with an anguish more intense than anything that accompanies his revelations about his own life. He understands his life as a model of the very creation that is beyond him and of course within him. He writes and writes, he reads and reads his way through the double conundrum, the linked mystery of his own biography and of creation.

He makes the central, paradoxical, discovery of autobiography: Memory is not in the service of the past; it is the future which commands its presence. Yet how bizarre the truncated modern notion of "seeking a self" would seem to Augustine. Autobiography for him does not seek a self, not even for its own salvation. For Augustine, the memory work of autobiography creates a self as the right instrument to seek meaning. The purpose is praise. If God, the source, the creator, is found, what else is there to do but praise?

Early in the *Confessions,* Augustine poses a problem that has a familiar modern ring: ". . . it would seem clear that no one can call upon Thee without knowing Thee." This is the problem of God's notorious absence. Augustine takes the next step West: He seeks his faith *with* his doubt. "May it be," he asks, "that a man must implore Thee before he can know Thee?" His assumption is that faith should not be confused with certainty. The only thing to count on is longing and the occult directives of desire. So, Augustine wonders aloud to God, does this mean prayer must come *before* faith? Perhaps not knowing is the first condition of prayer. Can that be?

Augustine finds his working answer in scripture: *"How shall they call on Him in Whom they have not believed? They shall praise the Lord that seek Him."* Longing is the only sure knowledge, that core of human instinct which unfurls its song of praise. This is the same center from which the narrative impulse of memory streams. Studying the meaning of Creation, Augustine discovers there is no way to escape the instinct to cry out this core truth which proves to be, quite simply, the wonder of a life lived. And, in the spirit of the Word, a life written.

*A*ugustine lived another thirty-three years after he wrote the *Confessions*. He remained Bishop of Hippo until his death in 430, and left a staggering amount of writing, sermons and letters, theological speculations and polemics, which he carefully annotated and archived. While some of his great theological treatises, notably the *City of God*, are available even today in paperback editions, only the *Confessions* has won the hearts of common readers century after century.

As an old man, Augustine set himself the project, rather like Henry James late in his life, of revising and remarking on each of his works. When he got to the *Confessions* he changed nothing. With quiet satisfaction and perhaps a hint of mild vindication, he said, as of a book which had already stood the test of time, that these thirteen books "concern both my bad and my good actions, for which they praise our just and good God. In so doing they arouse the human mind and affections toward him. As far as I am concerned, they had this effect upon me in my writing of them, and still do when I read them now. What others think about them is for them to say; but I know that they have given pleasure in the past, and still do give pleasure, to many of my brethren."

Augustine probably wrote this little memoir of his memoir in 427 or 428. He must have known that he and also the world he had described, the flourishing Roman civilization of worldly decadence and religious fervor he had struggled with so mightily in his book, were both close to death. Incredibly, Rome—eternal Rome, his gleaming Gotham—had fallen to barbarian attack in 410. Numidia, the backwater province of his birth which he had tried so desperately to escape, was now a rare remnant of the empire, still intact, still shining in the southern light he loved. During the final twenty years of his life, Augustine watched as refugees from the collapsing Roman world streamed into Africa with nothing but their broken lives, telling hair-raising tales of death and destruction. Rome, after all, came to him.

But not for long. Certainly he must have known that too. By the summer of 429 bands of Vandals were crossing from Spain, headed toward the African coast.

In August, 430, Augustine fell gravely ill. All his life, like the North African Berber that Monica was, he had been surrounded by others. His very way of life, an early monastic foundation, was based on the assumption of community. He had shared all his joys and struggles, even the most interior ones, with others, with his household of friends or with his fellow monks. Even his mystical moment at Ostia had not been a private affair: He and Monica had soared together. But now, in his last days, Augustine wanted to be left entirely alone.

He asked to have the penitential Psalms of David copied out and hung on the walls of his cell. For his last ten days, none of his brother monks was allowed to approach him. Outside, Vandal warriors were ravaging Numidia, nearing Hippo. A year later, the city would fall. But in these final days of life and of empire, Augustine gazed only at the Psalms, praying his way out of this world, merged at last into the Word which had been his greatest passion.

Reviewing
Anne Frank

*B*ook reviewing is the bread-and-butter labor of the writing life. In fact, it's considered hack work—though not by me. I have always been idealistic, even romantic, about reviewing. My affection may be rooted in the fact that writing book reviews was the first way I got published. Reviews provided the first sweet literary money I earned.

Fundamentally, literature is a conversation, strangely intimate, conducted between writer and reader—countless writers, unknown readers. Reviewing has never struck me as having much to do with assigning scores or handing out demerits. The reviewer's job—and pleasure—is akin to any reader's. It is the pleasure of talk. If nobody *talks* about books, if they are not discussed or somehow contended with, literature ceases to be a conversation, ceases to be dynamic. Most of all, it ceases to be intimate. It degenerates into a monologue or a mutter. An unreviewed book is a struck bell that gives no resonance. Without reviews, literature would be oddly mute in spite of all those words on all those pages of all those books. Reviewing makes of reading a participant sport, not a spectator sport.

But no assignment has been as daunting as the one given me to review the new "Definitive Edition" of Anne Frank's *Diary*. The *Diary* is a book like no other. For one thing, virtually all books assigned for review are just off the press. A reviewer is a kind of first reader, an explorer describing a new book, like a new country, to the people who have yet to travel there. But who does not know about Anne Frank and her heartbreaking diary? It was first published over fifty years ago, and has been translated into virtually every language in the world that sustains a book culture. Most readers know this book, like very few others, from childhood, and they carry it into adulthood.

Even if they haven't read it, people know the story and the essential personality of its extraordinary author. Besides the familiarity of the book, who on earth would claim to "review" Anne Frank? The book seemed to defy the very enterprise of book reviewing. I suppose the emotion ruling me as I approached my task was a paralyzing diffidence. Who was I to write about this icon of the Holocaust?

I procrastinated as long as I could. I did everything to keep from writing the review. I was very good at this. I read the book slowly, I underlined passages, I took notes, jotting down lines from the *Diary*, some of them passages I remembered with surprising sharpness from girlhood when I had first read the book, some of them new to me. The more I felt the power of the book, the more hopeless I felt. I missed the first deadline and called my editor, begging for an extension. Granted! A reprieve.

Then I procrastinated some more. I developed a sudden

urgency about cleaning my oven and sorting out my sock draw-er. I called friends, made lunch dates (I never go out to lunch when I'm working). I asked my friends what *they* thought about Anne Frank. I had a ferocious resistance to writing the review. I found yet another way to avoid writing which I could at least call "research": I dug up "The Development of Anne Frank," an essay about Anne Frank by John Berryman which I remembered having read or having heard about years before. I took notes on *that*.

I saw from a note in the text that the essay had been writ-ten in 1967. I had been Berryman's student at the University of Minnesota that year, taking two courses in "Humanities of the Western World" from him in a packed, overheated room with fifty or sixty other undergraduates. The room smelled of wet wool (our damp winter coats) and cigarette smoke (his unfiltered cigarettes which pitched perilously from his wildly gesticulating hand).

We understood Berryman was "a great poet." *Life* magazine had done a big picture story about him in Ireland, catching his Old Testament beard in the salt wind, the hand and the cigarette in motion against an abysmal sea. He talked about literature in a fierce, angry way, full of astonishment; he had an ability to bring a roomful of undergraduates to tears by reading aloud the farewell scene between Hector and Andromache in the *Iliad*. Mechanical engineering students, taking the class as a distribu-tion requirement, looked down with red, embarrassed faces, twisting their paperback Homers.

Berryman killed himself only a few years after I graduated. He jumped from a bridge on campus, a bridge I had walked across every day. I couldn't remember his ever saying anything about Anne Frank, but reading his essay about her all these years later brought him powerfully back, the force of his inquiring mind, his determination to understand what was at stake in her book, his assumption of the greatness of this little girl who kept a diary.

I still hadn't written a word.

But I had finally wandered into the task at hand. Though I ended up referring only briefly to a remark in Berryman's essay when I wrote my own review (a kind of private homage to him), it wasn't so much what his essay said that began to unlock my own timidity. Rather, it was the tone I felt in his essay, a voice that was so poised on *trying to understand* that it had no room for the kind of hand wringing I was indulging in myself.

Berryman began by telling how he had first come across Anne Frank's *Diary* in 1952 when the first installment of the translated text appeared in *Commentary* magazine. "I read it with amazement," he says in his essay. He was so galvanized by her writing that "the next day, when I went to town to see my analyst, I stopped in the magazine's offices . . . to see if proofs of the *Diary's* continuation were available, and they were." Then, "like millions of people later," he wrote, "I was bowled over with pity and horror and admiration for the astounding doomed little girl."

But he didn't stop with this emotional anchor. He demanded, right from the start, that he think as well as feel. "But what I *thought* was: a sane person. A sane person, in the twentieth century." Berryman had found the tip of his subject: How had such extraordinary sanity come to be developed in the crushing circumstances of Anne Frank's life which were the worst circumstances of the century? It wasn't necessary to remember the details of his own tragic end for me to feel his urgency in searching for "a sane person in the twentieth century."

I liked the naturalness of this beginning, the casualness of his saying he was "bowled over." I liked how, having established his feeling, he refused to dwell on it but pushed on to a thought. I could feel a mind at work, and more than that: I felt a story unfolding. He was writing a *story*, I suddenly thought, the story of his relation to this book. The ideas were like characters in the story that he kept looking at from one angle and then another in order to make sense of them, in order to come to a conclusion, much the way a story must bring its characters to some resolving, if mysterious, finale.

Strangely enough, it was at this point (if I remember correctly) that I made my first mark on paper, my first stab at my own response to Anne Frank. I wrote the first three paragraphs of my review, quite easily, as if there had been no procrastination, no moaning and groaning at all for several weeks of fretful false starts. After reading Berryman's essay, I knew what to do—at least for three paragraphs.

On Tuesday, March 28, 1944, Gerrit Bolkestein, Education Minister of the Dutch Government in exile, delivered a radio message from London urging his war-weary countrymen to collect "vast quantities of simple, everyday material" as part of the historical record of the Nazi occupation.

"History cannot be written on the basis of official decisions and documents alone," he said. "If our descendants are to understand fully what we as a nation have had to endure and overcome during these years, then what we really need are ordinary documents—a diary, letters."

In her diary the next day, Anne Frank mentions this broadcast, which she and her family heard on a clandestine radio in their Amsterdam hiding place. "Ten years after the war," she writes on March 29, "people would find it very amusing to read how we lived, what we ate and what we talked about as Jews in hiding."

No one, reading the opening paragraphs of John Berryman's essay about being bowled over and astonished to find in this little girl's diary "a sane person in the twentieth century" and then reading the opening of my review, which is a straightforward piece of historical information, would imagine that I had finally been nudged off the dime by his essay. Berryman's tone is personal and immediate. Mine is distanced (I never make use of the first person pronoun in my entire review) and rests its authority on certain historical facts I present to the reader dispassionately.

I got the hint about the Dutch Education Minister's clandestine radio message from the foreword to the "Definitive Edition," but I tracked down the exact quotation from the speech at the library. If I wasn't going to allow myself the kind of authority and presence that Berryman had with the use of the personal pronoun, I needed to achieve that sense of immediacy another way. Direct quotation from the minister's speech mimicked the clandestine wartime radio transmission.

I tried to make Anne Frank's knowledge of the minister's radio message part of this story—as indeed it actually was. I wanted the reader to see history happening as it happened for Anne Frank herself. That is why I began the review in a storylike way: "On Tuesday, March 28, 1944, Gerrit Bolkestein, Education Minister of the Dutch Government in exile, delivered a radio message from London urging . . ." In order to bolster the authority of this information in every way possible—and thereby to bolster the authority of my own narrative—I called the public library to find out what day of the week March 28 fell on in the year 1944 so that, casually, I could note that it was a Tuesday. I had to seduce the reader not with my emotional authority but with the authority of simple facts. A small thing, but words *are* small, and each one can count for a lot.

It is odd—even to me—that reading Berryman's very personal (though closely analytical) essay should have shown me the way into my own piece about Anne Frank. I had a number of constraints that hadn't hampered him. For one thing, I had much less space: My editor allotted me a certain number of words and no more. The reviewer's humble pie. Berryman had written an essay, a more open, luxurious form.

Still, many reviewers use the first person voice, and Berryman certainly had won me over partly because of his very immediate presence in his own essay. So why did I steer away from that voice? I think I understood, after reading Berryman's beautiful essay, the different task I had before me. What Berryman had done in 1967 didn't need to be done again. But I benefited from the freedom of his prose, the genuineness of his inquiry. It was a model for me—not a model of style, but of intention. I wasn't coming upon Anne Frank's *Diary* as it came out in proofs for the first time. I was responding to a definitive edition of a book that has long been a classic. I did not need to present myself as having been moved by the *Diary*. History had provided several generations of such readers. I needed to get out of the way.

Also, while I had been procrastinating by having lunch with my friends, one of my luncheon companions mentioned that there had been (and continues to be) an ugly, demented attempt to deny the authenticity of the *Diary*. Like many such anti-Holocaust theories, this one tries to prove that while there might have been a little girl named Anne Frank who had died during the war of "natural causes" (or in some versions had not died but been "lost" or who was herself a fabrication), this child had never written a diary. "The Diary of Anne Frank," these conspiracy theorists claim, was written by adults—by Anne Frank's father (whose presence as the sole survivor of his murdered family the theory does not account for) or by some others engaged in a "Jewish plot."

It was all quite mad.

The reason these allegations about the *Diary* had won any attention at all hinged on the fact that there are indeed several versions of Anne Frank's diaries. In preparing the first edition of the book, her father was compelled, partly by his own sense of discretion and partly by space limitations imposed on him by the original Dutch publisher, to make deletions. In 1986 a "Critical Edition" was published that meticulously presents Anne's original diary, plus the version she was working on for her proposed fictionalized version, "The Secret Annex," and the edition her father published—which is the edition all the world has come to know. The book I was reviewing was the restored, original diary, published for the first time in a reader's edition.

I studied the distinctions among the various texts carefully in the Critical Edition and attempted to present these distinctions briefly but clearly in a reference to the Critical Edition. This Critical Edition had been published in 1986 partly to refute the crazy allegations of the conspiracy theorists. I wanted to use my review, in part, to alert readers to any false claims made in this regard.

Berryman's essay made me powerfully aware of the time which had passed between his first response to the book in 1952, hardly seven years after Anne Frank's death in Bergen-Belsen, and my reading of the 1995 Definitive Edition when she would have been sixty-six. His task was to give the psychological project of the *Diary* its due. It was not yet clear, in 1967, that the *Diary* was a classic work of human development. Its very popularity had obscured, Berryman felt, its most important subject which was, he said, "even more mysterious and fundamental than St. Augustine's" in his *Confessions*: namely, "the conversion of a child into a person." My task was more modest. Beyond the basic biographical information which, for most readers, I knew would be unnecessary, I had to place the book in its public history.

With this in mind, I made reference at the end of the review to the book's age—fifty years old, and to Philip Roth's use of Anne Frank as a fictional character in his novel *The Ghost Writer*. I wanted to show how Anne Frank has entered our lives as a permanent presence, that to invoke her name is to invoke a person we know and who shall always be missing because her presence in her book has made her so alive it is "unthinkable and disorienting," as I say in my review, "to know that this life was crushed."

I remember feeling a kind of relief (not satisfaction, but the more unburdened feeling that the word "relief" suggests) when I stumbled upon the word "disorienting." For I felt this had something to do with the enduring grief and regret that mention of Anne Frank brings forward within us. My sense of being "disoriented" by her death was somehow related to Berryman's relief in finding a "sane person in the twentieth century." We *should* be disoriented by such hellish hatred. I was writing my review, after all, as children were dying from similar sectarian hatred in Bosnia. I too needed to find a sane person in the twentieth century. A child especially.

Finally, I wanted to remind people of the extraordinary person Anne Frank was, the splendid writer, the utterly natural girl/woman, and the gifted thinker. All my notes paid off, just as my luncheon with my friend had: I had many passages which I was able to use to present Anne Frank to readers not only as the icon of a murdered child but as the strong and vital writer she was. I came away from my reading of the *Diary* convinced absolutely that, had she lived, Anne Frank would have written many books and that we would know her not only as the author of her diary. And I came away with a clear answer to those sen-

timentalists who ask their appalling question: Would anyone really care about the diary if she hadn't died? Oh yes.

But maybe I always knew the answer to that question. When
I was a girl, first reading the *Diary,* I treasured it because Anne
fought and contended with her mother just as I did; she battled
to become a person—the very thing Berryman honored most in
her. I *needed* Anne Frank then—not because she was the child
who died and put a face on the six million murdered (I was not
yet capable of taking that in) but because, like me, she was determined to live, to grow up to be herself and no one else. She was,
simply, my friend. I don't think I was able to keep in mind that
she was dead. I went to her *Diary,* quite simply as she went to
Kitty, for a friendship not to be found anywhere else but in
books. As Anne Frank wrote to Kitty in a letter in her red plaid
notebook, "Paper is more patient than people." It is the secret
motto not only of a sensitive teenager but of any writer.

About two weeks after my review was published, I received
a small white envelope, addressed in a careful hand in blue ink,
forwarded to me from the *New York Times Book Review* which
had received it. There was no return address, but the envelope
was postmarked New York. A fan letter, I thought, with a brief
flutter of vanity.

Inside was a single sheet, my name written again with the
careful blue ink, and below that a crazy quilt of black headlines
apparently photocopied from various articles in newspapers and
periodicals. All of them claimed in their smudged, exclamatory
way to have evidence of the "Anne Frank Zionist Plot" or the
"Frank Lies." The headlines were all broken off and crammed
into one another; bits and pieces of the articles to which they
belonged overlapped. There wasn't a complete sentence on the
entire mashed and deranged page.

But there it was: The small insane mind responding spasmodically to the sane person John Berryman had been so relieved to discover as a middle-aged man, sick in his own mind and heart, the same sane person so many girls recognize as their truest friend as they move into the rough and beautiful terrain of womanhood.

I stood in my bright kitchen, holding that piece of paper, disoriented all over again. The paper literally felt *dirty,* perhaps because of the smudged typefaces. It was the sooty look of old-fashioned pornography.

I did with it the only thing possible: I burned it. Somehow it required burning, not just tossing out. I burned it in the kitchen sink, and watched the clotted ashes swirl down the garbage disposal.

My fury was mixed with something else—with disbelief, I think. I don't know what it will take to convince me of the world's capacity to hate life, its dark instinct to smash what blooms. Anne Frank knew this hard truth as a child. She refused to cave in to it even as she acknowledged it: "I hear the approaching thunder that, one day, will destroy us too, I feel the suffering of millions." The conversation she began with Kitty, her imaginary correspondent, was founded on a discipline of compassion. Even in acknowledging her own likely death, she felt not only for herself but felt as well "the suffering of millions." It made her into that extra thing—not a child, not a woman, but an artist.

This was the sane person who, John Berryman says at the end of his essay, "remained able to weep with pity, in Auschwitz, for naked gypsy girls driven past to the crematory. . . ." We seek her still, this sane person we long for at the end of our terrible century that tried so desperately to erase her.

The Need to Say It

My Czech grandmother hated to see me with a book. She snatched it away if I sat still too long (dead to her), absorbed in my reading. "Bad for you," she would say, holding the loathsome thing behind her back, furious at my enchantment.

She kept her distance from the printed word of English, but she lavished attention on her lodge newspaper which came once a month, written in the quaint nineteenth-century Czech she and her generation had brought to America before the turn of the century. Like wedding cake saved from the feast, this language, over the years, had become a fossil, still recognizable but no longer something to be put in the mouth.

Did she read English? I'm not sure. I do know that she couldn't—or didn't—write it. That's where I came in.

My first commissioned work was to write letters for her. "You write for me, honey?" she would say, holding out a ball-point she had been given at a grocery store promotion, clicking it like a castanet. My fee was cookies and milk, payable before, during, and after completion of the project.

I settled down at her kitchen table while she rooted around the drawer where she kept coupons and playing cards and bank calendars. Eventually she located a piece of stationery and a mismatched envelope. She laid the small, pastel sheet before me, smoothing it out; a floral motif was clotted across the top of the page and bled down one side. The paper was so insubstantial even ballpoint ink seeped through the other side. "That's OK," she would say. "We only need one side."

True. In life she was a gifted gossip, unfurling an extended riff of chatter from a bare motif of rumor. But her writing style displayed a brevity that made Hemingway's prose look like nattering garrulity. She dictated her letters as if she were paying by the word.

"Dear Sister," she began, followed by a little time-buying cough and throat clearing. "We are all well here." Pause. "And hope you are well too." Longer pause, the steamy broth of inspiration heating up on her side of the table. Then, in a lurch, "Winter is hard so I don't get out much."

This was followed instantly by an unconquerable fit of envy: "Not like you in California." Then she came to a complete halt, perhaps demoralized by this evidence that you can't put much on paper before you betray your secret self, try as you will to keep things civil.

She sat, she brooded, she stared out the window. She was locked in the perverse reticence of composition. She gazed at me, but I understood she did not see me. She was looking for her next thought. "Read what I wrote," she would finally say, having lost not only what she was looking for but what she already had pinned down. I went over the little trail of sentences that led to her dead end.

More silence, then a sigh. She gave up the ghost. "Put 'God bless you,'" she said. She reached across to see the lean rectangle of words on the paper. "Now leave some space," she said, "and put 'Love.'" I handed over the paper for her to sign.

She always asked if her signature looked nice. She wrote her one word—Teresa—with a flourish. For her, writing was painting, a visual art, not declarative but sensuous.

She sent her lean documents regularly to her only remaining sister who lived in Los Angeles, a place she had not visited. They had last seen each other as children in their village in Bohemia. But she never mentioned that or anything from that world. There was no taint of reminiscence in her prose.

Even at ten I was appalled by the minimalism of these letters. They enraged me. "Is that all you have to say?" I would ask her, a nasty edge to my voice.

It wasn't long before I began padding the text. Without telling her, I added an anecdote my father had told at dinner the night before, or I conducted this unknown reader through the heavy plot of my brother's attempt to make first string on the St. Thomas hockey team. I allowed myself a descriptive aria on the beauty of Minnesota winters (for the benefit of my California reader who might need some background material on the subject of ice hockey). A little of this, a little of that—there was always something I could toss into my grandmother's meager soup to thicken it up.

Of course, the protagonist of the hockey tale was not "my brother." He was "my grandson." I departed from my own life without a regret and breezily inhabited my grandmother's. I complained about my hip joint, I bemoaned the rising cost of hamburger, I even touched on the loneliness of old age, and hinted at the inattention of my son's wife (that is, my own mother who was next door, oblivious to treachery).

In time, my grandmother gave in to the inevitable. Without ever discussing it, we understood that when she came looking for me, clicking her ballpoint, I was to write the letter, and her job was to keep the cookies coming. I abandoned her skimpy floral stationery which badly cramped my style, and thumped down on the table a stack of ruled 8 1/2 x 11.

"Just say something interesting," she would say. And I was off to the races.

I took over her life in prose. Somewhere along the line, though, she decided to take full possession of her sign-off. She asked me to show her how to write "Love" so she could add it to "Teresa" in her own hand. She practiced the new word many times on scratch paper before she allowed herself to commit it to the bottom of a letter.

But when she finally took the leap, I realized I had forgotten to tell her about the comma. On a single slanting line she had written: *Love Teresa.* The words didn't look like a closure, but a command.

Write about what you know. This instruction from grade school was the first bit of writing advice I was ever given. Terrific—that was just what I wanted to do. But privately, in a recess of my personality I could not gain access to by wish or by will, I was afraid this advice was a lie, concocted and disseminated nationwide by English teachers. The real, the secret, commandment was *Write about what matters.*

But they couldn't tell you that, I sensed, because nothing

someone like me had experienced in the environs of St. Luke's grade school in Saint Paul, Minnesota, mattered to anybody, and such a commandment would bring the whole creaking apparatus of assignments and spelling tests crashing down. I was never able to convince myself that anyone wanted to know what I had done on my summer vacation. They were just counting on my being vain enough to be flattered into telling. And they were right. But I resented it, I resented having nothing—really—to write about.

Maybe I wouldn't have fretted over the standard composition advice if I had valued my life in a simple way. Or rather, if I had valued the life around me. But literary types are born snobs, yearning for the social register of significance. And I was a literary kid from the get-go, falling into fairy tales, and later, enormous nineteenth-century novels, as if into vats of imported heavy cream where I was perfectly content to drown.

I felt, I *believed,* my own life (and anything that touched it) was just so much still water. You could drown there too, but to no purpose, anonymous as a gasp, flailing around without experiencing the luscious sinking that made life worthwhile—which was literature. I wrote about princesses and angels. I filled in the silences left in familiar Bible stories, making up a travelogue about the flight into Egypt, fleshing out the domestic arrangements of Martha and Mary with a little dialogue: "'Don't you expect me to do those dishes, Martha,' huffed Mary. 'The Lord's on my side.'"

Later, I wrote about lesbians (though I wasn't one) and a demented arsonist (though I was afraid to use the fireplace at home). The beat went on: I was writing about things that mattered. That is, things beyond me.

Later still, inevitably, I gave up, and wrote about my own life after all, first in poems, and then in a memoir whose main figure was my Czech grandmother. She who commanded love. What bothers me about this brief history of my literary attempts is that I ended up writing memoir (even the poems were routinely autobiographical) when that was the last thing I wanted to do. Wasn't it?

And as a subplot to this conundrum, how was it that I rattled on with stories and descriptions of "what I knew" in those letters I wrote for my grandmother in her kitchen, and yet it never dawned on me that this was *writing*, that this was *it*.

Put another way: How did I come to believe that *what I knew* was also *what mattered*? And, more to the point for the future, *is* it what matters?

*M*aybe being oneself is always an acquired taste. For a writer it's a big deal to bow—or kneel or get knocked down— to the fact that you are going to write your own books and not somebody else's. Not even those books of the somebody else you thought it was your express business to spruce yourself up to be. The recognition of one's genuine material seems to involve a fall from the phony grace of good intentions and elevated expectations. (I speak from experience, as memoirists are supposed to.)

A hush comes over the writing, an emotion akin to awe: So, something just beyond my own intelligence seemed to whisper when I began writing about my grandmother's garden which I couldn't imagine anyone caring about, it isn't a matter of whether you *can* go home again. You just do. Language, that most ghostly kind of travel, hands out the tickets. It never occurred to me, once given my ticket, to refuse it.

Yet, it wasn't the ticket I wanted. I didn't want to go home, I wanted to go—elsewhere. I wanted to write novels. Fat ones.

Later, thinner ones—having moved from George Eliot to Virginia Woolf in my reading. But novels. About love and betrayal among grown-up modern men and women who should have behaved better (I thought). An important subject (I believed). A subject not given its due by men writers (I attested).

Instead, I've written memoir. And, so far, precious little love and betrayal of the sort I aspired to. Would that I could say that it's because I never experienced any betrayal along the way to or from love. But the equation between life and art hasn't proved to be so simple.

Still, I begin to see the elegance of a mathematical law in this confusion of impulse and execution, of intention and finished product: The material I was determined to elude has claimed me, while the subjects I wished to enlist in my liberation have spurned me.

Shame seems to be an essential catalyst in the business. Item: When I started college at the University in Minneapolis, I lost no time dumping the Catholic world my family had so carefully given me in Saint Paul. In fact, that's why I went there: I understood many people had succeeded in losing their religion at the University. I didn't miss a beat turning down a scholarship at a Catholic college where I had been assured I would get more "individual attention." Who wanted individual attention? I wanted to be left alone to lose my soul.

For years, decades even, I considered it one solid accomplishment that I had escaped the nuns. Result: I spent the better part of five years writing a memoir about growing up Catholic, a book which took me for extended stays at several monasteries and Catholic shrines in Europe and America. The central character of the book: a contemplative nun, the very figure I was determined to dodge.

Item: I was ashamed (though I didn't know it, couldn't have

called it shame) that my Czech grandmother couldn't write English, that she was who she was at all. An immigrant is a quaint antecedent at a distance; mine was too close for the comfort of my literary ambition. The shame was real, disloyal, mean. Result: She came and got me, and became the heroine of my first memoir. She wrote it first: *Love Teresa*. And I did, finally.

Subject matter is only half the story. It may be possible to trace the lines leading to and from a writer's life and art in an attempt to reveal why someone writes about this and not about that. But form is a tougher nut: Why a memoir, why not a novel?

I still puzzle over the reason I write books that deny me the pleasure of changing point of view, for instance. And admiring the straight spine of plot that gives the novel its grand carriage, why have I consorted with a flabby genre with the habit of dithering aimlessly, fingering its pressed flowers from the recumbent swoon of reminiscence?

The memoir comes in for a lot of heat. It is accused of being a notorious bore, of betraying the beady mind of a grudge-bearer. Even the name—memoir—sounds lightweight, a designer genre with too much cheesy pastel between the lines. Invoking memoir is even a standard way of dismissing a bad novel: It's merely autobiographical.

For a while, I took refuge in the belief that at least memoir had the decency to make a fair contract with the reader. The prose promised no more and no less than it paid out: my mother, my father, my childhood, my perception of it all. No overreaching omniscient narrators here. I grabbed the notion of honesty and hung on.

Then, a couple of years ago, a friend (a novelist, of course) ruined things. She had just read aloud from a novel she was working on. The reading was a hit, and everyone, including me, crowded around to praise her. The car ride to the family cabin which opened the book was especially strong; I could smell the pine needles, I told her. "Oh good," she said, a little shy, "that was our drive every year when I was a girl."

"Did you ever think of writing it as a memoir?" I said. It was an idle question, but it caught her off-guard.

"Oh no, I wouldn't write it as a memoir," she said, obviously repelled. "I want to tell the truth."

She looked embarrassed for an instant. It was purely social embarrassment, though; she was startled by her unvarnished candor in the face of the memoirist before her. She quickly recovered her novelist self, and looked right at me, her keen dark eyes holding their judgment: She wanted to tell the truth of her life— and memoir, she saw, doesn't encourage the truth.

She was not troubled by memory's habit of embracing the imagination. Long before, she had put her faith in the revelation of detail, not the accumulation of fact. Neither one of us was looking for a way to make literature a spreadsheet. The truth she felt memoir denied her was not the public truth of history or scholarship or journalism.

She mistrusted memoir because it would not allow her to speak her soul's truth. Paradoxically, memoir allowed less intimacy than fiction. Writing directly from her life did not provide fiction's freedom to tell the truth derived from family secrets, from intensely personal events, from the burnt but still blooming core of the self. Memoir was left to explore the trivial—or to falsify the real. Or perhaps, its lowest sin: To make a mean little case against the past (aka, mother and father). I brooded on all that. I brood still.

Yet I wrote—I write—memoir. I had come to accept the inevitable tango of memory and imagination. I even looked forward to their inescapable encounter. It became one of the sharper pleasures of writing memoir: How uncanny to go back in memory to a house from which time has stolen all the furniture, and to find the one remembered chair, and write it so large, so deep, that it furnishes the entire vacant room. The past comes streaming back on words, and delivers the goods it had absconded with.

For all of that deep pleasure of retrieval, memoir is not about the past. As I understand it, memoir is not a matter of nostalgia. Its double root is in despair and protest (which, at first, seem no more kissing cousins than memory and imagination).

The despair comes from the recognition, impersonal but experienced as intensely intimate, that all things die. Not only individual, ordinary lives (all of them, of course, all of *us*), but whole civilizations, rafts of accomplishments, gestures, moments. Even the proper rage and horror at gigantic evil get eroded over time into conventional pieties. Nothing lasts, not even the solemn oath to remember.

The mind never gets over this betrayal of experience. In its dismay, memory allies itself with the larger political and social sensibility around it, the consciousness that makes people A People, a nation. This is the consciousness that causes the oppressed to take final refuge in culture, the consciousness that makes them willing to die—and kill—for a culture.

Out of the dread of ruin and disintegration emerges a protest which becomes history when it is written from the choral voice of a nation, and memoir when it is written from a personal voice. The dry twigs left of a vanished life, whatever its fullness once was, are rubbed together until they catch fire. Until they make something. Until they make a story.

Looked at this way, the truth memoir has to offer is not neat-ly opposite from fiction's truth. Its methods and habits are dif-ferent, and it is perhaps a more perverse genre than the novel: It *seems* to be about an individual self, but it is revealed as a minion of memory which belongs not only to the personal world but to the public realm. As such, the greatest memoirs tend to be aller-gic to mere confession and mistrustful of revenge, though these are two of the genre's natural impulses.

This refusal of memoir to display successfully raw confession or revenge is not, I'm sure, evidence of its inability to sustain per-sonal truth. In fact, I like the mongrel nature of the genre that combines traits of fiction and of the essay, and lets just about any-body into the club. I'm content to sit on the same bench with aging movie stars, with wistful sons of powerful men who seem to know they'll never amount to much even though they've kicked their cocaine habit, with abused daughters trying to get back at sleazy fathers.

The memoir is not just a rest home for sensitive souls. Poets purveying acute angles of vision are there next to successful plaintiffs in palimony suits, and people whose fate has drawn them to Patagonia or away from Romania.

It's a quirk of the memoir that its narrator can never be its hero. Once again, it seems that memoir prefers the cooler, more neutral, term. The narrator is the protagonist—not the hero.

I'm used to being a protagonist by now, though that was not my original intention. No doubt, I'd write a very unconvincing heroine. I wonder if I'd even know how.

*W*riting about why you write is a funny business, like scratching what doesn't itch. Impulses are mysterious, and explaining them must be done with mirrors, like certain cunning sleight-of-hand routines. All the while I've been trying to grasp the reason I have written what I have in the manner I have; I've been working those mirrors for all they're worth.

Off to the side the whole time, in my lateral sight, has been a single snapshot which I'm convinced possesses the complete explanation. How like a memoirist to believe a solo image, fluttering in the dark, is the rare butterfly that will, at last, complete the collection.

But I am a memoirist, so I'm off with my net: I'm in the sixth grade (blue serge uniform jumper, white blouse with Peter Pan collar). I'm still sitting in the second-to-last desk, in the row next to the windows. In a few months I will be moved forward, seat by seat, at my own troubled request until it is finally discerned that I need glasses.

But right now, I am still in that blessed outer region far from the blackboard and Sister's desk, still in the slight slur of undiagnosed myopia. And Mike Maloney who doesn't love me (he *likes* me, he has said, making that distinction for me for the first time) sits behind me. We're pals. He is whispering something funny at the back of my head. That's gone forever.

Then Sister asks a question. I'd give a lot to know now what that question was. It's gone forever too, and I'm having a much harder time letting it go. Because I know the answer to this question. It's a really tough question and I just know nobody else in that class has the answer.

I've heard people talk about their hearts being in their throats, but I feel this extraordinary sensation—my *mind* or my brain or whatever is *me* is in my throat. I'm throbbing with the answer to that question, and my arm shoots up. It's waving crazily. I look like a drowning person grasping for help. But really I'm a bird, mighty with song. Sister has to call on me, I'll die if I can't crow out the answer. I reach to her, way from the back, my mad hand jumping.

She scans the room, *doesn't see me,* and turns to the board with her chalk. And provides the answer herself, just doles it out like medicine we all should take. And goes on with the lesson.

The throbbing in my throat actually hurts. My soul thuds inside me. Tears squint in my eyes from the raw denial I've been dealt. I'm aware, somewhere, that this whole thing is odd. But the main thing is, it's real. And I've got the answer and I've still got the wild need to say it.

I look out the window. We're on the third floor, and I see, below on the far playground, the other sixth-grade class at recess. I think I can make out Tommy Schwartz in his faded cords and plaid shirt and Sheila Phalen, wearing exactly what I am wearing. She is my best friend, we walk to school together; he is a basketball star, I adore him. Sheila alone knows this.

What are they doing together? I will never know. But his head is bent slightly toward her. A new kind of misery enters me.

They're far away, I can barely make them out. Maybe it's not Tommy after all. But I've already pasted dreamy smiles on their faces. I squint, but that only blurs things. I have no desire to turn and talk to Mike Maloney who is right there behind me, and who likes me.

No. I want to communicate with those little indistinct figures way off there, who may or may not be Tommy and Sheila, who may or may not be pressing the first valentine of love and betrayal into my palm, who may not even care that I have the answer. But I can't get rid of the ache in my throat which I know is my brain. I'll burst if I can't give my answer, that's all I know for sure.

Other People's Secrets

The river is still now. Nighttime, and I have come here to sit alone in the dark in the wooden boat under its canvas roof, to tally up, finally, those I have betrayed. Let me count the ways. Earlier, white herds of cloud, way up there and harmless, buffaloed across the sky. A beautiful day, and everyone, it seemed, was on the water.

But now the pleasure craft that tooled back and forth all day, plying the marina's no-wake zone, are gone. Only a flotilla of linked barges rides high and empty, headed downriver to Lock Number Two at Hastings, intent on the river's serious business. The massive lozenges look strangely sinister as they part the dark water. By day these barges seem benign—riverine trucks, floating grain or ore or gravel between Saint Paul and the great Elsewhere. But now they pass by spectrally, huge and soundless.

Spotlights from the county jail send wavering columns of moon-colored light across the water from that side of the river to the marina on this side. I once saw a woman, standing on the Wabasha Bridge, lean as far over the guardrail as she could, and blow kisses toward the jail while traffic rushed around her. I followed her gaze and saw a raised arm clad in a blue shirt, indistinct and ghostly, motioning back from a darkened window. The loyal body, reaching even beyond bars to keep its pledge.

The boat groans in its slip, the lines that hold it fast strain as they absorb the wake from the barges. Boat, dock, ropes rub companionably against each other, sending out contented squeaks and low, reassuring moans that sound as if they're saying exactly what they mean—*tethered, tethered.*

This is the location in between, not solid land, not high seas. Just a boat bobbing under a covered slip, the old city of my life laid out before me—the cathedral where my parents were married, the great oxidized bulb of its dome looking like a Jules Verne spaceship landed on the highest hill of the Saint Paul bluffs; on the near shore of Raspberry Island, an elderly Hmong immigrant casting late into the night for carp poisoned by PCBs; and downtown, in the middle distance, the bronze statue of the homeboy, Scott Fitzgerald, a topcoat flung over his arm even in summer, all alone at this hour in Rice Park, across from the neoclassical gray of the Public Library where it all began for me. "You'll like this place," my mother said, holding my hand as we entered—impossible luck!—a building full of books.

Let's start with mother, then, first betrayal.

It was all right to be a writer. In fact, it was much too grand, a dizzy height far above the likes of us. "Have you thought about being a librarian instead, darling?" At least I should get my teaching certificate, "to fall back on," she said, as if teaching were a kind of fainting couch that would catch me when I swooned from writing. But I knew I mustn't take an education course of any kind. Some wily instinct told me it is dangerous to be too practical in this life. I read nineteenth-century novels and Romantic poetry for four years, and left the university unscathed by any skill, ready to begin what, already, I called "my work."

I knocked around a jumble of jobs for ten years, working on the copy desk of the Saint Paul newspaper, recording oral histories in nursing homes around town—Jewish, Catholic, Presbyterian. I edited a magazine for the local public radio station. I lived in a rural commune on nothing at all, eating spaghetti and parsley with others as poetry-besotted as I, squealing like the city girl I was when a field mouse scurried across the farmhouse floor. I went to graduate school for two years—two more years of reading poetry. A decade of this and that.

Then, when I was thirty-two, my first book was accepted for publication, a collection of poems. My mother was ecstatic. She wrote in her calendar for that June day—practically crowing— "First Book Accepted!!" as if she were signing a contract of her own, one which committed her to overseeing an imaginary multiple-book deal she had negotiated with the future on my behalf.

She asked to see the manuscript out of sheer delight and pride. My first reader.

And here began my career of betrayal. The opening poem in the manuscript, called "Mother/Daughter Dance," was agreeably imagistic, the predictable struggle of the suffocated daughter and the protean mother padded with nicely opaque figurative language. No problem. Only at the end, rising to a crescendo of impacted meaning, had the poem, seemingly of its own volition, reached out of its complacent obscurity to filch a plain and serviceable fact—my mother's epilepsy. There it was, the *grand mal* seizure as the finishing touch, a personal fact that morphed into a symbol, opening the poem, I knew, wide, wide, wide.

"You cannot publish that poem," she said on the telephone, not for once my stage mother, egging me on. The voice of the betrayed, I heard for the first time, is not sad. It is coldly outraged.

"Why not?" I said with brazen innocence.

Just who did I think I was?

A writer, of course. We get to do this—tell secrets and get away with it. It's called, in book reviews and graduate seminars, courage. *She displays remarkable courage in exploring the family's. . . . the book is sustained by his exemplary courage in revealing . . .*

I am trying now to remember if I cared about her feelings at all. I know I did not approve of the secrecy in which for years she had wrapped the dark jewel of her condition. I did not feel she *deserved* to be so upset about something that should be seen in purely practical terms. I hated—feared, really—the freight she loaded on the idea of epilepsy, her belief that she would lose her job if anyone "found out," her baleful stories of people having to cross the border into Iowa to get married because "not so long ago" Minnesota refused to issue marriage licenses to epileptics. The idea of Iowa being "across the border" was itself absurd.

She had always said she was a feminist before there was feminism, but where was that buoyant *Our Bodies, Ourselves* spirit? Vanished. When it came to epilepsy, something darkly medieval had bewitched her, making it impossible to appeal to her usually wry common sense. I rebelled against her horror of seizures, though her own had been successfully controlled by medication for years. It was all, as I told her, no big deal. Couldn't she see that?

Stony silence.

She was outraged by my betrayal. I was furious at her theatrical secrecy. Would you feel this way, I asked sensibly, if you had diabetes?

"This isn't diabetes," she said darkly, the rich unction of her shame refusing my hygienic approach.

Even as we faced off, I felt obscurely how thin my reasonableness was. The gravitas of her disgrace infuriated me partly because it had such natural force. I was a reed easily snapped in the fierce gale of her shame. I sensed obliquely that her loyalty to her secret bespoke a firmer grasp of the world than my poems could imagine. But poetry was everything! I knew that. Her ferocious secrecy made me feel foolish, a lightweight, but for no reason I could articulate. Perhaps I had, as yet, no secret of my own to guard, no humiliation against which I measured myself and the cruelly dispassionate world with its casual, intrusive gaze.

I tried, of course, to make *her* feel foolish. It was ridiculous, I said, to think anyone would fire her for a medical condition— especially her employer, a progressive liberal arts college where she worked in the library. "You don't know people," she said, her dignified mistrust subtly trumping my credulous open-air policy.

This was tougher than I had expected. I changed tactics. Nobody even reads poetry, I assured her shamelessly. You have nothing to worry about.

She dismissed this pandering. "You have no right," she said simply.

It is pointless to claim your First Amendment rights with your mother. My arguments proved to be no argument at all, and she was impervious to any blandishment.

Then, when things looked lost, I was visited by a strange inspiration.

I simply reversed field. I told her that if she wanted, I would cut the poem from the book. I paused, let this magnanimous gesture sink in. "You think it over," I said. "I'll do whatever you want. But Mother . . ."

"What?" she asked, wary, full of misgivings as well she might have been.

"One thing," I said, the soul of an aluminum-siding salesman rising within me, "I just want you to know—before you make your decision—it really is the best poem in the book." Click.

This was not, after all, an inspiration. It was a gamble. And though it was largely unconscious, still, there was calculation to it. She loved to play the horses. And I was my mother's daughter; instinctively I put my money on a winner. The next morning she called and told me I could publish the poem. "It's a good poem," she said, echoing my own self-promoting point. Her voice was rinsed of outrage, a little weary but without resentment.

Describe it as I saw it then: She had read the poem, and like God in His heaven, she saw that it was good. I didn't pause to think she was doing me a favor, that she might be making a terrible sacrifice. This was good for her, I told myself with the satisfied righteousness of a nurse entering a terrified patient's room armed with long needles and body restraints. The wicked witch of secrecy had been vanquished. I hadn't simply won (though that was delicious). I had liberated my mother, unlocked her from the prison of the dank secret where she had been cruelly chained for so long.

I felt heroic in a low-grade literary sort of way. I understood that poetry—my poem!—had performed this liberating deed. My mother had been unable to speak. I had spoken for her. It had been hard for both of us. But this was the whole point of literature, its deepest good, this voicing of the unspoken, the forbidden. And look at the prize we won with our struggle—for doesn't the truth, as John, the beloved apostle promised, set you free?

Memory is such a cheat and privacy such a dodging chimera that between the two of them—literature's goalposts—the match is bound to turn into a brawl. Kafka's famous solution to the conundrum of personal and public rights—burn the papers!—lies, as his work does, at the conflicted heart of twentieth-century writing, drenched as it is in the testimony of personal memory and of political mayhem.

Max Brod, the friend entrusted to do the burning, was the first to make the point in his own defense which has been taken up by others ever since: Aside from the unconscionable loss to the world if he had destroyed the letters and the journals with their stories and unfinished novels, Brod, as his good friend Kafka well knew, was a man incapable of burning a single syllable. Kafka asked someone to destroy his work whom he could be sure would never do so. No one seriously accuses Brod of betraying a dying friend. Or rather, no one wishes to think about the choice in ethical terms because who would wish he had lit the match?

But one person did obey. Dora Diamant, Kafka's final and certainly truest love, was also asked to destroy his papers. She burned what she could, without hesitation. She took Kafka at his word—and he was alive to see her fulfill his command. She was never wife or widow, and did not retain any rights over the matter after Kafka's death, but even Brod, Kafka's literary executor, felt it necessary to treat her diplomatically, as late as 1930, and to present his case to her when he set about publishing the work.

As she wrote to Brod during this period when they tried to come to an understanding about publication of Kafka's work:

The world at large does not have to know about Franz. He

is nobody else's business because, well, because nobody could possibly understand him. I regarded it—and I think I still do so now—as wholly out of the question for anyone ever to understand Franz, or to get even an inkling of what he was about unless one knew him personally. All efforts to understand him were hopeless unless he himself made them possible by the look in his eyes or the touch of his hand. . . .

Hers is the austere, even haughty claim of privacy, a jealous right, perhaps. She knew it: "I am only now beginning to understand . . . the fear of having to share him with others." This, she freely admits to Brod, is "very petty." She does not claim that her willingness to destroy the work was a wholly noble act. She is surprisingly without moral posturing.

Still, she could not bear to give the world those works she had not destroyed. As Ernst Pawel says in *Nightmare of Reason: A Life of Franz Kafka,* she denied that she had them until, after her marriage to a prominent German Communist, their house was raided by the Gestapo in 1933 and every piece of paper, including all the Kafka material, was confiscated, never to be located to this day. She was, finally, distraught, and as Pawel says, "confessed her folly" to Brod.

Pawel, an acute and sensitive reader of Kafka and his relationships, puzzles over this willful act of secrecy. "The sentiment or sentimentality that moved this otherwise recklessly truthful woman to persist in her lie," he writes, clearly perplexed, ". . . may somehow be touching, but it led to a tragic loss."

Yes—but. The lie Dora Diamant persisted in was a simple one—her refusal to admit to Kafka's editors or friends that she still possessed any of his papers. But her letter to Brod (written three years before the Gestapo raid) is not the document of a woman who is simply "sentimental." She is adamantly anti-literary. The papers she refused to hand over—and which, terrible irony, were swept away by the Gestapo into that other kind of silence, the wretched midcentury abyss—were, no doubt quite literally to her, private documents. After all, most of Kafka's works were written in—or as—journals. There is no more private kind of writing. The journal teeters on the edge of literature. It plays the game of having its cake and eating it too: writing which is not meant to be read.

The objects Kafka asked Dora Diamant to destroy and those she later refused to hand over to editors did not have the clear identity of "professional writing" or of "literature." They were works from a master of prose writing, but they were still journals and letters. They must have seemed, to her who had lived with them, intensely personal documents. If it is understood even between lovers that a journal is "private," off limits, not to be read, it doesn't seem quite so outrageous that Dora Diamant, who loved the man, would choose to honor his privacy as she did. In fact, it is not a mystery at all, but quite in keeping with her character as a "recklessly truthful woman."

Privacy and expression are two embattled religions. And while the god of privacy reigns in the vast air of silence, expression worships a divinity who is sovereign in the tabernacle of literature. Privacy, by definition, keeps its reasons to itself and can hardly be expected to borrow the weapons of expression—language and literature—to defend itself. To understand the impulse of privacy that persists against every assault, as Dora Diamant's did, her position must not call forth the condescension of seeing her adamant refusal as being merely "touching."

In her 1930 letter to Brod, Dora Diamant is trying to express what she maintains—against the institutional weight and historical force of literature—is a greater truth than the truth that exists in Kafka's papers. She is determined to remain loyal to his appalling absence and to the ineffable wonder of his being, "the look in his eyes," "the touch of his hand."

This is not sentimentality. She speaks from a harsh passion for accuracy—nothing but his very being is good enough to stand as his truth. Literature at best is a delusion. It is the intruder, the falsifier. She makes an even more radical claim—it is unnecessary: "The world at large does not have to know about Franz." Why? Because their "knowing"(possible only through the work now that he is dead) is doomed to be incomplete and therefore inaccurate. A lie, in other words. In her terms, it is a bigger lie, no doubt, than her refusal to admit to those eager editors that she did indeed have the goods stashed away in her apartment.

No writer could possibly agree with her. Except Kafka, of course. But maybe Kafka wasn't "a writer." It may be necessary to call him a prophet. In any case, Dora Diamant wasn't a writer. She belonged to the other religion, not the one of words, but the human one of intimacy, of hands that touch and eyes that look. The one that knows we die, and bears silently the grief of this extinction, refusing the vainglorious comfort of literature's claim of immortality, declining Shakespeare's offer:

> So long as men can breathe or eyes can see,
> So long lives this, and this gives life to thee.

The ancient religions all have injunctions against speaking the name of God. Truth, they know, rests in silence. As Dora Diamant, unarmed against the august priests of literature who surrounded her, also knew in her loneliness: What happens in the dark of human intimacy is holy, and belongs to silence. It is not, as we writers say, material.

*T*here is no betrayal, as there is no love, like the first one. But then, I hadn't betrayed my mother—I had saved her. I freed her from silence, from secrecy, from the benighted attitudes which had caused her such anguish, and from the historical suppression of women's voices—and so on and so forth. If Dora Diamant was someone who didn't believe in literature, I was one who believed in nothing else.

This defining moment: I must have been about twelve, not older. A spring day, certainly in May because the windows and even the heavy doors at St. Luke's School are open. Fresh air is gusting through the building like a nimble thief, roller shades slapping against windows from the draft, classroom doors banging shut. The classrooms are festooned with flowers, mostly drooping masses of lilac stuck in coffee cans and Mason jars, placed at the bare feet of the plaster Virgin who has a niche in every classroom: *Ave, ave, Ma-ree-ee-ah,* our Queen of the May.

For some reason we, our whole class, are standing in the corridor. We are waiting—to go into the auditorium, to go out on the playground, some everyday thing like that. We are formed in two lines and we are supposed to be silent. We are talking, of course, but in low murmurs, and Sister doesn't mind. She is smiling. Nothing is happening, nothing at all. We are just waiting for the next ordinary moment to blossom forth.

Out of this vacancy, I am struck by a blow: *I must commemorate all this.* I know it is just my mind, but it doesn't feel like a thought. It is a command. It feels odd, and it feels good, buoyant. Sister is there in her heavy black drapery, also the spring breeze rocketing down the dark corridor, and the classroom doorway we are standing by, where, inside, lilacs are shriveling at the bare feet of Mary. Or maybe it is a voice that strikes me,

Tommy Howe hissing to—I forget to whom, "OK, OK, lemme go."

These things matter—Tommy's voice, Sister smiling in her black, the ricochet of the wind, the lilacs collapsing—because I am here to take them in.

That was all. It was everything

I have asked myself many times about that oddly adult word—*commemorate*—which rainbows over the whole gauzy instant. I'm sure that was the word, that in fact this word was the whole galvanizing point of the experience because I remember thinking even at the time that it was a weird word for a child—me—to use. It was an elderly word, not mine. But I grabbed it and held on. Perhaps only a Catholic child of the fifties would be at home with such a conception. We "commemorated" just about everything. The year was crosshatched with significance—saints' feast days, holy days, Lent with its Friday fasts and "Stations of the Cross." We prayed for the dead, we prayed *to* the dead.

How alive it all was. Commemoration was the badge of living we pinned on all that happened. Our great pulsing religion didn't just hold us fast in its claws. It sent us bounding through the day, the week, the month and season, companioned by meaning. To honor the moment, living or dead, was what "to commemorate" meant. This, I sensed for the first time, was what writers did. Of course, being a Catholic girl, I was already sniffing for my vocation. Sister was smiling, her garments billowing with the spring wind, and here was "the call," secular perhaps, but surely a voice out of the whirlwind.

*T*he sense of the fundamental goodness of the commemorative act made it difficult to believe "commemoration" could be harmful. Beyond this essential goodness I perceived in the act of writing, I felt what I was up to was a kind of radiance, a dazzling shining-forth of experience. I never liked the notion that writers "celebrated" life—that was a notion too close to boosterism and the covering-over of life I thought writers were expressly commissioned to examine. But who could be hurt by being honored—or simply noticed? Who could object to that?

A lot of people, it turned out. My mother was only the first. "You can use me," a friend once said, "just don't abuse me." But who, exactly, makes that distinction?

"You're not going to *use* this, are you?" someone else asked after confiding in me. She regarded me suddenly with horror, as if she had strayed into a remake of *Invasion of the Body Snatchers,* where she played a real human who has just discovered I'm one of *them.*

Later, I strayed into a scary movie myself. I'd become friendly one year with a visiting writer from one of the small, indistinct countries "behind the Iron Curtain," as we used to say. It was a year of romantic upheaval for me—for her too. God knows what I told her. We met for coffee now and again, and regaled each other with wry stories from our absurdist lives. Then she went back where she had come from.

A year later I received in the mail a book in a language completely unknown to me. When I saw her name on the cover I realized this was the book she had been writing in Minnesota. "Just wanted you to have my little American book!" the cheery note said. An American publisher was interested in releasing an English translation, she added. I flipped through the incomprehensible pages. Suddenly, two hideous words cleared the alphabet soup with terrible eloquence: *Patricia Hampl.* Then I saw, with increasing alarm, that my name—me!—popped up like a ghoulish gargoyle throughout the text, doing, saying, I knew not what.

"I don't think you'll be too upset," someone who could read the incomprehensible language told me, but declined to translate. "It's a little sticky," she said vaguely. Sticky?

Later still, at a workshop with a Famous Novelist, I raised my hand and posed the question. "You've said in interviews that your fiction is autobiographical," I began, notebook ready to take down his good counsel. "I'm wondering what advice you might have on writing about family or close friends?"

"Fuck 'em," he said. And I shivered the body-snatcher shiver. So you *do* have to become one of them?

Over the years, as other books followed my first, I told the story of how I had spoken for my mother who could not speak for herself. I had all my ducks lined up in a row—my belief in the radiance of the commemorative act, my honorable willingness to let my mother decide the fate of the poem, her plucky decision to let me publish the poem which at first she had seen as a cruel invasion but which—the real miracle—she came to recognize was nothing less than a liberation for her. She and I, together, had broken an evil silence. See what literature can do?

Then one day I got a call from a poet who was writing a piece about "personal writing." She had been in an audience where I had told my mother-daughter story—there had been many by this time: I had my patter down. It was a wonderful story, she said. Could she use it in her essay as an example of . . .?

The words "wonderful story" hung above me like an accusation. The blah-blah-blah of it all came back and stood before me, too contemptuous even to slap me in the face. I felt abashed. I told her I wanted to check the story first with my mother.

She answered the phone on the first ring. She was still working, still at her library job. *Remember that poem in my first book,* I said, *the one that has the seizure in it and you and me?*

Oh yes.

Remember how I told you I wouldn't publish it if you didn't want me to, and you said I could go ahead?

Yes.

Well, I was just wondering. Is that something you're glad about? I mean, do you feel the poem sort of got things out in the open and sort of relieved your mind, or—I sounded like a nervous teenager, not the Visiting Writer who had edified dozens of writing workshops with this exemplary tale—*or* . . .

What *was* the or? What was the alternative?

Or did you just do it because you loved me?

Without pausing a beat: *Because I loved you.*

Then the pause: *I always hated it.*

Bobbing again on the water in the old boat, still in between. A nightly ritual, but now, as if on cue for the climax, lightning has begun to knife the sky, and thunder has started its drumrolls. Hot summer night, waiting to break open the heat, and spill.

No wonder I like to come down here, this floating place. I was attracted too to the in-between position of the writer. More exactly, I was after the suspended state that comes with the act of writing: not happy, not sad; uncertain of the next turn, yet not lost; here, but really *there*, the there of an unmapped geography which, nonetheless, was truly home—and paradisal.

The elusive pleasure to be found in writing (and only *in* it, not the *before* of anticipation, not the *after* of accomplishment) is in following the drift, inkling your way toward meaning. My old hero, Whitman, that rogue flaneur, knew all about it: "I'm afoot with my vision!" he exulted. It was an *ars poetica* I too could sign up for, basking in the sublime congruence of consciousness "afoot" in the floating world.

There are, it is true, memoirists who are not magnetized by memory. They simply "have a story to tell." They have the goods on someone—mother, father, even themselves in an earlier life, or on history itself. "Something" has happened to them. These stories—of incest or abuse, of extraordinary accomplishment or exceptional hardship, the testimonies of those who have witnessed the hellfire of history or the anguish of unusually trying childhoods—are what are sometimes thought of as the real or best occasions of autobiography.

Memory, in this view, is a minion of experience. It has a tale to tell. Its job is to witness the real or to reveal the hidden. Sometimes the impulse to write these accounts is transparently self-serving or self-dramatizing. But at least as often, and certainly more valiantly, this is the necessary literature of witness. Historic truth rests on such testimony. The authority of these personal documents is so profound, so incriminating, that whole arsenals of hatred have been arrayed in mad argument for half a century in a vain attempt to deny the truth of a little girl's diary. These kinds of memoir count for a lot. Sometimes they are the only history we can ever hope to get.

Still, memory is not, fundamentally, a repository. If it were, no question would arise about its accuracy, no argument would be fought over its notorious imprecision. The privacy of individual experience is not a right as Dora Diamant tried to argue with Max Brod, or as my mother begged me to see. Not a right, but something greater—it is an inevitability that returns no matter what invasion seems to overtake it. This privacy is bred of memory's intimacy with the idiosyncrasy of the imagination. What memory "sees," it must regard through the image-making faculty of mind. The parallel lines of memory and imagination cross finally and collide in narrative. The casualty is the dead body of privacy lying smashed on the track.

Strangely enough, contemporary memoir, all the rage today as it practically shoves the novel off the book review pages, has its roots not in fiction which it appears to mimic and tease, but in poetry. The chaotic lyric impulse, not the smooth drive of plot, is the engine of memory. Flashes of half-forgotten moments flare up from their recesses: the ember-red tip of a Marlboro at night on a dock, summer of '54, the lake still as soup, or a patch of a remembered song unhinged from its narrative moorings— "*Glow little glow worm, glimmer, glimmer,*" and don't forget the skinned knuckle—Dad's!—turning a dead ignition on a 20-below winter day. Shards glinting in the dust.

These are the materials of memoir, details that refuse to stay buried, that demand habitation. Their spark of meaning spreads into a wildfire of narrative. They may be domesticated into a story, but the passion that begot them as images belongs to the wild night of poetry. It is the humble detail, as that arch memorialist Nabokov understood, which commands memory to speak: "Caress the detail," he advised, "the divine detail." And in so doing, he implicitly suggested, the world—the one lost forever—comes streaming back. Alive, ghostly real.

Kafka called himself "a memory come alive." His fellow townsman, Rilke, also believed that memory, not "experience," claims the sovereign position in the imagination. How strange that Kafka and Rilke, these two giants who preside as the hieratic figures, respectively, of The Writer and The Poet for the modern age, were both Prague boys, born barely eight years apart, timid sons of rigid fathers, believers in the word, prophets of the catastrophe that was to swallow their world whole and change literature forever. Canaries sent down into the mine of history, singing till the end.

In *Letters to a Young Poet,* the little book it is probably safe to say every young poet reads at some point, Rilke wrote to a boy who was a student at the very military academy where he himself had been so notoriously miserable. He wrote, no doubt, to his younger self as well as to this otherwise unknown student poet, Franz Zaver Kappus. Though the boy was only nineteen, Rilke sent him not forward into experience, but deeply inward to memory as the greatest "treasure" available to a writer.

"Even if you found yourself in some prison," Rilke says in the first letter, "whose walls let in none of the world's sounds—wouldn't you still have your childhood, that jewel beyond all price, that treasure house of memories."

This is not an invitation to nostalgia—Rilke had been painfully unhappy as a boy, stifled and frightened. He was not a sentimentalist of childhood. He is directing the young poet, rather, to the old religion of commemoration in whose rituals the glory of consciousness presides. He believes, as I cannot help believing as well, in the communion of perception where experience does not fade to a deathly pale, but lives evergreen, the imagination taking on the lost life, even a whole world, bringing it to the only place it can live again, reviving it in the pools and freshets of language.

I have gone to visit my mother. She is in the hospital, has been there now many weeks. "It's hell to get old," she says, barely voiced words escaping from the trach tube from which she breathes. Almost blind, but still eager to get back to her E-mail at home. She smiles from her great charm, a beatific smile, when I say "E-mail," when I say "home." There is a feeding tube in her stomach. There was a stroke, then her old nemesis, a seizure, a heart attack, respiratory this, pulmonary that—all the things that can go wrong, all the things that have their high-tech solutions. She is surrounded by beeps and gurgles, hums and hisses. She'll get home. She's a fighter. At the moment, fighting her way out of the thick ether of weeks of sedative medicines.

She is glad I have come. She has been, she tells me, in a coffin at Willwersheid's Mortuary. Terrible experience, very confining.

I tell her she has not been in a coffin, I assure her she has not been at a funeral parlor. I tell her the name of the hospital where she is.

She looks at me as at a fool, not bothering to conceal her contempt. Then the astonishing firmness that kept me in line for years: *I have been in a coffin. Don't tell me I have not been in a coffin.*

Well, I say, you're not in a coffin now, are you?

No, she says, agreeing with vast relief, *thank God for that.*

The trip, she says animatedly, trying to express the marvel of it all, has been simply *amazing.* Shipboard life is wonderful. Skirting Cuba—that was beautiful. But the best part? The most beautiful, wonderful black woman—a real lady—came to her cabin with fresh linens. The ironing smelled so good! That was what made Port-au-Prince especially nice. People everywhere, she says, have been so lovely.

Why not? It's better than the coffin at Willwersheid's. Then, the air, saturated by weeks of medication, suddenly clears, and we're talking sensibly about people we know, about politics—she knows who's running for governor, and she wouldn't vote for Norm Coleman if he were the last man on earth. We see eye to eye. She asks about my father, she asks about my work—our usual subjects.

"Actually," I say, "I'm writing about you. Sort of."

She's in a wheelchair, the portable oxygen strapped to the

back. We have wheeled down to the visitors' lounge and are looking out the big picture window that has a view of the capital building and the cathedral, and even a slender curve of the Mississippi in the distance where I will go when I leave here, to sit again to brood in the little boat under the canvas slip. She can see the capital and the cathedral. Storms grizzle the sky with lightning, and her good eye widens with interest.

I say I am trying to tell the story again of the poem about the seizure. "I'm trying to explain it from your point of view," I say.

She nods, takes this in. "Yes," she says slowly, thoughtfully. "That's good you're doing that finally. It's very important to . . . to my career." Her smile, the great rainbow that the nurses have remarked on, beams in my direction, the wild sky behind us, flashing.

Her career. Yes. Her own passage through this life, the shape she too has made of things, her visions, the things she alone knows. The terrible narrowness of a coffin and the marvels of Port-au-Prince, the astonishing kindness of people, the pleasure of sweet-smelling linen. I can see now that she was standing up for the truth of her experience, the literal fact of it, how it jerked and twisted not only her body but her life, how it truly *seized* her. My poem and I—we merely fingered the thing, casually displaying it for the idle passerby. What she knows and how she knows it must not be taken from her.

I never understood the fury my desire to commemorate brought down upon me. The sense of betrayal—when I thought I was just saying what I saw, drawn into utterance, I truly believed, by the buoyancy of loving life, all its strange particles. I didn't have a dark story of abuse to purvey or even a horde of delicious gossip. I was just taking pictures, I thought. But then, doesn't the "primitive" instinct know that the camera steals the soul? My own name skittering down the pages of a foreign book, sending alarms down my spine. The truth is: The constraining suit of words rarely fits. Writers—and readers—believe in the fiction of telling a true story. But the living subject knows it as the work of a culprit.

Years ago, when I was living in the poetry commune, eating spaghetti and parsley, I had a dream I knew would stay with me. A keeper, as my father says of fish. I was behind the wheel of a Buick, a big improbable Dad car I couldn't imagine driving in real life. I was steering with my eyes shut, traveling the streets of my girlhood—Linwood, Lexington, Oxford, even Snelling with its whizzing truck traffic. It was terrifying. I understood I must not open my eyes. And I must not turn the wheel over to the man sitting beside me in the passenger seat though he had his eyes wide open. If I wanted to reach my destination (murky, undefined), I must keep driving blind. My companion kept screaming, "You'll kill us all!"

I've lost quite a few people along the way. And not to death. I lose them to writing. The one who accused me of appropriating her life, the one who said he was appalled, the poet miffed by my description of his shoes, the dear elderly priest who said he thought I understood the meaning of a private conversation, this one, that one. Gone, gone. Their fading faces haven't faded at all, just receded, turned abruptly away from me, as is their right.

I have the letters somewhere, stuffed in a file drawer I never open. The long letters, trying to give me a chance to explain myself, the terse ones, cutting me off for good. The range of tone it is possible for the betrayed to employ—the outrage, the disgust, the wounded astonishment, the quiet dismay, the cold dismissal. Some of them close friends, some barely known, only encountered. All of them "used," one way or another, except for the baffling case of the friend who wrote to complain because I had *not* included her.

Mother and I are safe inside, staring out the big hospital window as our city gets lost in sheets of gray. "Is it raining?" she asks. The storm is wild, bending old trees on Summit Avenue, snapping them easily, taking up clots of sod as they go down. Down at the river the boat must be banging against the dock.

My mind scrolls up the furious swirl of phrases in those letters from people who no longer speak to me. And me, surprised every time. *"I cannot believe that you would think . . ."* *"Maybe it seemed that way to you, but I . . ."*

But I'm getting too close again, hovering at their sides where they don't want me, trying to take down the dialogue. Better not. Leave the letters in their proud silence. No quotes, no names. Or else, someone, in a dream or elsewhere, is likely to rise up in fury, charging with the oracular voice of the righteous dead that I've killed again.

Acknowledgments

"Memory and Imagination" originally appeared in *The Dolphin Reader II* (Houghton Mifflin, 1986) and has been reprinted extensively in anthologies, including, most recently, *The Anatomy of Memory,* edited by James McConkey (Oxford University Press).

"The *Mayflower* Moment: Reading Whitman during the Vietnam War" originally appeared in the anthology *Walt Whitman: the Measure of His Song* (Holy Cow! Press, 1981).

"The Smile of Accomplishment: Sylvia Plath's Ambition" originally appeared in *The Iowa Review,* 1995.

"A Book Sealed with Seven Seals: Edith Stein" originally appeared in the anthology *Martyrs,* edited by Susan Bergman (Harper Collins, 1996).

"Czeslaw Milosz and Memory" originally appeared in *Ironwood* magazine, 1981, and has been revised since the post-Communist revolutions in Eastern Europe.

"The Need to Say It" originally appeared in *The Writer on Her Work II,* an anthology edited by Janet Sternburg (W. W. Norton, 1991).

"The Invention of Autobiography: Augustine's *Confessions*" first appeared as the preface to the Vintage Classics of Spirituality edition of *The Confessions* (1998).

"Other People's Secrets," originally appeared in *The Business of Memory,* edited by Charles Baxter (Graywolf Press, 1999).

Credits